"Halfway through my own journey into invisible, not known, not recognized, alienated visible, a recognized authority in my field, valued, connected, daring, I would say this: Read this book before you pen on paper. Al Bargen and Nick Brodd wrote this book with you in mind and left no stone unturned. My favorite chapter is when Al and Nick show us how to write your book without trying so hard! They have a noble mission right here, right now: to make you Visible, Known, Recognized, Valued, Connected, Daring. Absolutely brilliant!"

–Marina Nani,
Double-Award Winning Author of *Away from Home* and *The Simple Truth* series
www.AwayFromHome-Book.com

"If you have always wanted to have a book published but felt daunted by the task, this is the book for you. I have met a lot of people who were confident about their writing but were put off by all the other things they would need to learn to achieve it. This book breaks the process down into achievable chunks and gives practical advice about how to outsource the parts you don't want to do yourself. So don't delay. Buy this book and take the first step towards publishing your book."

–Pat Duckworth
Award-Winning Author of *Hot Women, Cool Solutions*
www.RoystonHypnotherapy.co.uk

"The tips and strategies in *Hard Core Soft Cover* are critical to anyone looking to write their book, whether they are a first-time author or seasoned writer. Nick and Al's cure for writers block and their technique for rapidly developing your book outline will ensure you have a book published within weeks as opposed to the months or even years you imagined it takes."

–Charles Bodi
Results and Success Coach
www.CharlesBodiTeam.com

"I definitely recommend this book to everyone out there who wants to write his own book. Where was this book when I started working on mine last year? Now thanks to Nick and Al, I have an entire process I can use to help me get back to my project and get my book done."

–Chantal Sauvé
Success and Transformational Coach
www.ChantalSauveCoaching.com

"This book shouldn't look like any other book because it's not. Why? There is not a single page wasted in this book. Nick and Al have filled it to the brim with writing advice, tips and insights that any person who wants to write a book, be it his first, second or third book, will find extremely valuable. I was getting blocked on my second book and this drop-kicked me right into fifth gear! Look, bottom line, do you want to write better, faster and more efficiently, all while improving your ability to draw in the reader to want to invest time in your book? Then this book is your next book, period."

–Pete Asmus
Investor, Author and Radio Talk Show Host
www.C2CReia.com

"Informative, encouraging and inspiring are the three words I would use to describe *Hard Core Soft Cover*. This book makes the process of writing a book clear and easy to follow. The information is delivered in a fun, easy-to-understand style, making it possible for anyone with a message to write a book. I found that this book filled in the missing links for my own writing process, which enabled me to get back to writing with passion. Well done!"

–Oceanna Rivers
Soul Exploration Coach
www.ExploreWithin.ca

"Nick and Al have a winner in *Hard Core Soft Cover*! If writing a book is on your bucket list, but you've been putting it off because you just don't know where to start, here's your answer. I love how you're taken by the hand and led step by step through the process, and guided past all the hurdles that may otherwise put your book on hold. Nick and Al thought of every detail, and did it in an easy to read, easy to implement way. Do yourself a favour and read this book before you start your own."

–Dan Giercke
Author of *Create Your Legacy Fortune and Stealth Wealth*
www.MoneyMentorAcademy.com

"Always wanted to write a book but you let fear hold you back? Problem solved. In Al Bargen & Nick Brodd's *Hard Core Soft Cover,* you are guided through the whole process from beginning to end. Nick and Al makes it easy and they make you realize that FEAR stands for False Evidence Appearing Real. This is a must-read for anyone who ever dreamt of writing his own book but did not know where to start. Kudos to the authors."

—Anita Telle
Award-Winning Author of *A Little Different All Perfect*
www.Boo-BooBear.org

"It was great to get an advanced copy of this book. I have just started to put my own manuscript together, and will definitely use this information"

—Matt L.
Kelowna, BC

"Nick and Al combine not just their experience in writing, but they were wise enough to draw on the experience of many bestselling authors. That's what creates the magic secret sauce in this book. Use it as your recipe to success in your writing endeavors."

–Robin P.
Edmonton, AB

Published by:
Writers Rise
Kelowna, British Columbia
Web: WritersRise.com

HARD
CORE
SOFT COVER

CREATE YOUR HARD-HITTING FAST-SELLING BOOK IN
— 30 HOURS OR LESS —

NICK BRODD AND AL BARGEN

This book is dedicated to you,
who came here with the courage and drive
to write your first book.

"What an astonishing thing a book is. It's a flat object made from a tree with flexible parts on which are imprinted lots of funny dark squiggles. But one glance at it and you're inside the mind of another person, maybe somebody dead for thousands of years. Across the millennia, an author is speaking clearly and silently inside your head, directly to you. Writing is perhaps the greatest of human inventions, binding together people who never knew each other, citizens of distant epochs. Books break the shackles of time. A book is proof that humans are capable of working magic."

–Carl Sagan

Contents

WRITING PHASE

Chapter 9: Whip Your Research into Shape

Chapter 10: Rapid Writing

Chapter 11: How to Open Your Book with a Proverbial Bang

Chapter 12: Embrace Your Inner Critic Now!

Chapter 13: Title Writing 101

Chapter 14: How to Sleep

Chapter 15: Going Hard-Core!

Acknowledgement

Silent gratitude is of no use, which is why we would like to publicly thank the many people who helped us reach this point.

Dr. John Gray, we are inspired to know someone who has sold more than 50 million books. Thank you for teaching us that the best way to reach out to our clients is to open our hearts to them. **Raymond Aaron**, for your wisdom that helped us get our book to market, and especially for your advice on branding. Podcasting superstar **Pat Flynn**, for being the living, breathing proof that nice guys don't finish last, and for teaching us how to be more productive writers. **Jay Papasan**, for showing us that millionaires, whether real estate agents or not, start with a clear goal in mind. **Cathy Presland**, for impressing upon us that there is no better time to write a book than now. **Connie Ragen Green**, for your information on marketing and attracting the right clientele. And to **David Shiang**, for imparting your knowledge on becoming a successful online entrepreneur.

Nicole, for helping us polish our manuscript. **Rahul**, for your impressive renditions of our mascot, Peter Pen, and for the illustrations that helped make this book come to life. And **Rachmad**, for creating the best cover for this book.

And of course, to our beautiful wives, **Aseel** and **Helena**, for the unwavering love, support and the sandwiches you make for us when we're busy writing. And to our children, Nick's **David** and **Angelina** and Al's **Brandon**. You guys aren't old enough to see this yet. But when you grow up, you will know that seeing you smile is always what melts all our stresses away.

And, of course, to all our fellow authors we converse with on a regular basis. To be able to bounce off ideas with you is truly a blessing.

We cannot thank you all enough.

Welcome, Future Author!

An Introduction to the Book Writing Process

The moments that change our lives are rarely the moments we expect. For me, it happened on a scorching afternoon in the Okanagan Valley in British Columbia, Canada.

I was alone at my desk, frustrated again. The project I was working on had been dragging on and on. It should have been finished by now. Actually, it should have been finished last year. It had been a goal of mine to record my thoughts, strategies, tips and tricks on fat loss and exercise and put everything into a book. My own book. It had been my goal for many years. But all I had to show for it were a couple of boxes filled with unkempt notes and exercise programs and a few random Word documents on my computer desktop.

With my head between my hands and my seeming defeat getting the best of me, I strained to find a reason not to give up my goal. Other than this was what I had always wanted, I could not find any other justification to continue. I just had no idea what to do. You could say I was on the verge of giving up. So I turned on the TV to see a replay of an MMA match. The fighters were ripped. I remembered the incredibly hard-core training programs of the MMA fighters I've had the privilege of training with. And then, it hit me. Was there also a hard-core method for writing a book? What if there was something that would give rapid results?

That was when it finally occurred to me, on that very same scorching afternoon in the Okanagan, British Columbia, that I should not be embarking on this massive journey to write a book without some type of direction. What I needed was a coach, someone who had been where I was before and had already figured out all the pitfalls. Someone who could direct and guide me from falling into one of those traps that prevented me from achieving the awesome goal of teaching people the very same thing I do to maintain single-digit body fat and my six-pack abs and still eat many cheeseburgers over the weekend. I needed someone to help me write my own soft cover book in a hard-core way.

I was determined to find the right book writing coach. And I was extremely privileged to have found Raymond Aaron, *New York Times* bestselling author of *Chicken Soup for the Parent's Soul* and a host of other books. After doing what Raymond asked me to do, I felt as though a massive weight was lifted off my shoulders. I was making progress. Rapid progress. Within a very short period of time, I was holding my book in my hands. I can still remember the day the first books arrived at my doorstep. I took the first copy and signed it over to my amazing wife, Helena. I wrote a very mushy, sappy message inside the front cover and handed it to her. Her eyes welled up with tears when she read what I had written. It was definitely one of the prouder moments in my life. And I knew, from the way she looked at me, that she was very proud of me too.

It was amazing to hold my first book in my hands. What I find even more amazing is how much easier this second book came along compared to the first. Obviously, years were not spent preparing and repeating mistakes. This time, things were streamlined. This time, the progress was much more rapid and, frankly, without as much frustration. In fact, the progress was so rapid that the only way I can describe the way this second book came together is exhilarating. I can only imagine what the third one has in store, now that I know how to write a book in less than 30 hours.

We will all leave something behind when we die. I'm happy to be able to leave a book in my name. Books with super solid, hard core content will survive for generations. They hit the market hard and sell fast in the short run. But, more importantly, they leave behind a legacy far beyond your spouse and children. Books allow you to uplift humanity now and for future generations.

Al,
Fitness Enthusiast, Nature-Lover, Husband and Father

The Making of *Hard Core Soft Cover*

Around the same time Al was working on his first book, I kept retouching my own. It was not easy and it certainly was not quick. It took me three months writing the final draft. Before that, I had already spent more than a year fine-tuning the presentation notes that were to become the base for the manuscript. Unlike Al, I had no coach. I had decided to take on the writing of my very first book on my own. Looking back now, I can see how much time and energy I lost singlehandedly working on something that was best done with a partner.

When Al and I committed ourselves to writing this book, we both had learned our lessons. We learned how to use our time more wisely, enabling us to write better books in a shorter span of time. But we were up for a challenge. We haven't reached the *New York Times* bestsellers list yet, and our first books took us way too long to finish. We knew we were ahead of the first-time authors who hadn't written any books yet, but, relatively speaking, we still had fairly limited experience.

And then, one day, Al asked the right question whose answer would bring us to where we are today: "How do we get the knowledge we need?"

The answer was obvious. As a management consultant and business executive, I rapidly learned that the fastest and most effective way to gain knowledge and experience is to learn first-hand from people who already have a lot of experience doing what you want done. We quickly decided that we needed to tap into the minds of the very best authors the world has to offer. We had to reach out to bestselling authors who have a proven track record of writing hard-hitting, fast-selling books, books that have exceptionally valuable content—the kind of content that sells.

So I took on the task of contacting and interviewing the giants of the publishing industry. The results were ground-breaking for us. We knew there were a lot of opportunities for improving our work, but if I hadn't learned directly from the masters, I would probably have been skeptical of what's possible.

Believe it or not, this book, which is my second book, took me just around 30 hours to complete. I spent maybe 10 hours preparing and then drafting a very extensive outline and feeding it with key concepts we wanted to explain. Then I spent five hours maximum on getting in touch with established authors and experts and interviewing them for this book. Then another five hours communicating with AI to brainstorm and share ideas and updates on the progress of tasks. The rest of the time was spent on writing, editing and polishing our final draft.

Writing a book quickly is not about working harder. It's not even about working longer hours each day. It's about working smarter. I don't have rare superpowers that allow me to write this fast. When I say I did all of this in 30 hours, and that you can do it in even less time, I'm not taking it lightly.

First of all, Swedish is my mother tongue, not English. Second of all, I'm not a born writer. I don't have natural writing talents of any sort. In fact, most of my school teachers would probably be surprised if they saw this book with my name on it. And third, I'm a perfectionist and a slow reader. It takes me a long time to proofread, way more time than the average person does. But the fact is hard and clear. I got this book written in 30 hours. By the end of this book, you'll learn how to do the same in even less time. Because effective writing is not so much about talent as it is about using the hard-core tactics, strategies, techniques and tools. I've proven that.

One thing that a lot of people tell me is they don't think their books will come out well if they cram all the work in 30 hours or less. That is most definitely not true. When reading this book, I encourage you to judge the quality of the writing for yourself. The truth of the matter is I could never have written this book in 30 hours without an editor. In fact, it would have taken me many, many, many more hours. We want to be completely transparent here. Al and I own Writers Rise, a publishing company that offers editing services. You could say we are a little biased about getting an editor. But the fact remains that we couldn't have done it without one.

When I tell people I had little say on the quality of writing of my book, I always get confused stares. I understand the confusion. This is probably the first time people have given the idea any thought. Other than assembling an exceptionally awesome support team, I've done very little to make sure my thoughts get massaged, smoothed and polished until it sounded perfect to my ears. And our promise to you is throughout this book we will share simple tricks that will allow you to build a support team of your own, with editors and project managers like Al, which doesn't cost a fortune.

We always want rapid results in everything we do. When it comes to writing a book, results aren't always as swift as we want them. This makes it even more valuable to get quick outcomes. Rapid results give you more time to do what you love and spend time with your family and loved ones. It will also enable you to generate more income. After all, once your book is launched and is selling, you've created a passive income stream. With the ability to write books rapidly, you can start setting up multiple streams of income faster than you may have imagined.

So when you write your books, we ask you not to make the same mistakes we did. Don't waste years trying to figure it out on your own. Instead, simply follow the steps outlined in this book, steps that came from some of the most brilliant minds and bestselling authors of our lifetime. When you do, it will only be a month, or even a couple of weeks, before you'll be holding your first book in your hands.

Nick
Business Executive, Productivity Champion, Family Man

A Rundown of the Writing Process

Writing a book is not a piece of cake, but it certainly is something that can be done if you know what you are doing and if you find the right people to help you. If writing suddenly becomes seemingly impossible, it is only because you are not aware of the people you need to get in touch with to get the job done.

Writing, and writing a whole book for that matter, is not simply sitting down in front of your computer and typing away on the keyboard until you come up with your very own masterpiece. Writing is a process that is divided into three general phases. These phases are further divided into more specific tasks that we are going to tackle one by one. The following are the three general phases of writing a book:

1. The Preparation Phase

2. The Research Phase

3. The Writing Phase

The Preparation Phase sets you up for writing. If you have never written a book before, you might assume that writing is putting down the words as they come. You let them flow when they are in your head and get stuck when inspiration won't come. This is a haphazard way of writing because you're writing a book on the whim of your muse. If you're stuck, you're stuck. There is no other way for you to move ahead except by looking out the window at the clear blue sky to wait for inspiration to come back. This is not the way authors do the job. Creative people do need more time

To conduct research is to widen your perspective on the subject and build upon other people's ideas to add to the current discourse.

and space to sort out their thoughts. However, this is different from idly waiting for the parts of your book to arrange themselves together. In the Preparation Phase, you will learn everything you need to know to make sure that you come up with a book that serves your purpose, whether that purpose is to make money, build a brand or simply share information. You will learn how to set yourself up so that you have a clear, definable target and an open path towards that target.

The next phase is the Research Phase. Research is a vital part of the writing process. Some people ask why they still have to do research if they already know the topic so well. Research doesn't simply provide you with more information that you can add into your book. It facilitates the rise of deeper insights and better ideas to add more value for your readers. Research is by no means stealing other people's ideas. Stealing is a crime. It is the biggest crime any author can ever commit. Research is simply widening your perspective on the subject and building upon other people's ideas to add to the current discourse.

Also, better research means less effort coming up with what to write about. The human brain's capacity to generate ideas is hard-core. But our conscious minds can only do so much without getting help from other sources. Ideas do not normally pop out of thin air. They are often the result of revising, simplifying and merging other ideas we have consciously or unconsciously gathered from somewhere else. The more you get from research, the faster your brain combines those pieces of information together and the earlier you will finish your book.

The last phase is the Writing Phase. Just because it comes last doesn't mean it is the easiest or quickest part. Actually, the bulk of the work goes into the Writing Phase. This is the part where you go hard-core into the next level and sit down in front of your computer to put all the words and sentences together. But it doesn't end there. When you reach the last page, you will still have to go through everything to make sure your content is accurate, your style is engaging and your grammar is flawless. So, in truth, writing actually means writing the first draft then the second draft then the third draft, and maybe even a fourth and a fifth draft until you're completely sure your book is ready to be published.

The entire process doesn't have to be done in a linear way. If you're already in the Writing Phase and you feel as though you need more material to support a certain chapter, it's perfectly fine to go back to the Research Phase to gather more information. Or if you think that your target readers will not be able to easily connect with your content, feel free to take a few steps back and rethink what you really want to say.

All of this may sound overwhelming to you. It is if you look at the book writing process like the Great Wall of China. No matter how hard you try, you won't be able to tear it down. Fortunately, we have powerful and effective tools that will help you take down those ancient bricks one by one. And it won't take you years to do that. In a matter of hours, you will have blasted your own hole into the giant wall, through which you can easily come and go.

In this book, you will learn how to break down the massive process of book writing and turn it into simple, manageable and doable tasks that you can tackle one at a time. By the time you finish reading this book, you will be equipped with the right knowledge and the confidence to take your idea and transform it into an enjoyable, information-rich non-fiction book that will sell.

In a Nutshell: The Three Crucial Concepts You Will Learn from This Book

1. You will learn how to set a clear purpose for your book and make sure you're always on the right track towards your objective.

2. You will learn how to gather information and generate ideas at almost lightning speed so you don't run out of things to write.

3. You will learn the quickest, easiest way to have a book written from page 1 to 300, or until the last word is put to paper.

PREPARATION PHASE

2

Why Am I Doing This Again?

How to Write a Book With a Clear Purpose in Mind

Why do you want to write a book? It's a simple question that a lot of people who say they want to write a book cannot answer. People write because they want to tell the world something. They want to share information and ideas they know will be useful to a certain kind of reader. There are just some things that are better communicated in words than in pictures, movies or sound. But why does it need to be a book? Why don't you just write a blog, a newspaper article or a Facebook post?

Different people have different goals when they write a book. It doesn't matter what your goal is as long as you stick to it all the way through. For you to get a clear view of your goal, take a step back and look at the bigger picture. Don't just aim to write 100,000 words and publish it as a book. Look way beyond writing the book and visualize the results you want to accomplish.

For our Writers Rise podcast, we interviewed Jay Papasan, publishing executive and co-author of the bestselling book *The Millionaire Real Estate Agent*. One thing Jay shared with us that helped us write a better book was to write it with its purpose always in mind. "When we set out to write *The Millionaire Real Estate Agent*," he said, "It was the first book that we worked on together. We had a very clear business purpose behind this: We wanted to put our company on the map with the top agents."

It might sound like New Age self-help babble for you to create a purpose, but it is one of those crucial little tasks that provide a jump-off point for your writing. Without a purpose in mind, you won't be able to create a clear writing plan and follow it. The only way you can doggedly commit to writing a book is to know why you are doing it in the first place. You know what a writer with no purpose is like? He's like a traveller with no destination. He wanders around aimlessly for years until he decides it's time to choose a direction. Are you ready to create your purpose?

Good, let's get down to it then. Take out a piece of paper and think about what you would like to happen after you finish writing your book. Be specific about what you want. We all want our books to sell well or to boost our credibility, but in what ways do you want to make money from your very first book? What kind of treatment do you want to receive from other people once they learn that you are an author? Different people have different takes on what they want to happen following the publication of their books. Some desires common to most authors are the following:

1.   Increase your income.

Writing a book is a great way to create profit. For a lot of successful authors, it's one way to build multiple streams of income. As long as the information you provide is useful and properly marketed, people will always want to buy your book. This makes a good book a lucrative income stream that can last a good long while until people decide they no longer need the information you provide. And there is no reason for you to stop after your first book. The approach we are going to share with you makes the writing process extremely manageable. Once you get your first book down pat, it will be even easier for you to move to the next book, and the next book and the next book. One by one, you will develop multiple streams of income.

2.   Create a brand for yourself.

Having a book with your name on it can help you build your own personal or business brand. A good book can serve as a platform for your brand. If you are at all serious about your brand, and of course you should be, consider at least having a book or two to your name.

If you write a lackluster book with nothing new to offer, you are making a lousy brand for yourself. Al has learned so much about branding from Raymond Aaron, who also wrote *Branding Small Business for Dummies*. We are passing all this knowledge on to you through our Writers Rise blog. The gist of it all is that writing a book to create a brand is all about creating powerful content that people find useful and interesting. It's all about establishing you as the expert. People will come to you to ask questions and solicit your opinion because, by reading your book, they know that you know your stuff. You don't offer fluff. You only offer rich material that people can use in their daily lives.

3.   Raise your visibility and credibility.

A well-written book with your name as the author tells people one thing: You're an expert. You're an authority. People can rely on you, whether for information or for products or services that your business offers.

Growth strategist and entrepreneur Cathy Presland, author of *Get Momentum Guide to Starting a Business: 30 Days to Turn Your Inspiration to Income*, says, "This moment is so critical because there's just so much credibility attached to having a book. I've done this where I've given talks and I stand there and I have my iPad and say, 'This is my book.' I stand at the front and people are in awe of the fact that I have

You can write a book to add more assets to your income stream. As long as you provide useful, interesting and relevant information, people will keep buying your book.

completed a book." When you write a book, you're putting yourself out there for public scrutiny. And that is when people start to take you seriously.

4.   Improve your website traffic.

Writing a book naturally gives your website, if you have one, a rapid traffic rise. People flock to you because they either want more information or they want to do business with you. Either way, you get better search rankings and, very possibly, an even bigger boost to your income stream. All those benefits you gain without you having to do additional work. And even when you prefer to distribute your book for free, your website still gains substantial traffic increases when you distribute the book through all the right channels, such as social networking websites, niche forums and file-sharing websites.

5.   Stand out from your competition.

Whether you're aiming to be promoted to the corner office at work or get a few more customers for your business, having a book under your name will certainly attract the attention of the right people. It will separate you from the sea of sameness that is your competition. When the promotions officer asks you why he should pick you instead of the other fellow who seems incredibly qualified for the position, wouldn't having a book published about a topic that's relevant to the position give you an edge?

Imagine yourself at a party. What would it be like to tell people that you have authored a book? You would probably get a small crowd gathering around you. Or you would probably get introduced to everybody at the party. People will naturally come to you because they trust you. And they trust you because you have demonstrated your worth by authoring a book.

6.   Market your business.

Internet shopping has forced consumers to make more intelligent choices. We no longer simply take things at face value and believe whatever advertisers want us to believe. People want to know more about a product or service they are buying before they whip out their credit cards. What easier way to satisfy your customers' need for information than to present everything in book format?

Businesses used to employ cold calling and other torturous techniques to get to their customers. Now, smart business people no longer hit the streets to knock on doors. Among several other things they do, they roll out a helpful book that readers can use to educate themselves about the product or service they're interested in. Sometimes, the book is offered for free in exchange for the reader's email address. At the end of the book, if the content was able to persuade the reader that the product or service is useful, easy-to-use or helpful enough to be bought, the reader can go to the product link and proceed to the checkout counter. That's marketing without having to go through rejections 90% of the time.

7.   Help other people.

A book worth reading is a book that helps other people. The ideas you share and the stories you tell can reach people who need help, inspiration and guidance to do something with their lives. You can do something as small as teaching them how to cure a minor ailment without going to the doctor or as big as inspiring them to turn their lives around. It doesn't matter how big or small of an impact you make. More often, the littlest things can cause the biggest changes. Your book can be just what your readers are looking for. If so, then it's time to write it.

You can choose to write a book solely for the purpose of earning money. Or you can do so simply to share your knowledge. The truth, however, is that you will most likely gain all of the benefits of authoring a book mentioned above, whether you intentionally want to have these benefits or not. Still, it is important that you choose exactly which one single purpose you want to work towards. Decide what your ultimate goal is and write your book with that goal in mind.

In fact, don't just decide that purpose to yourself. The thought that you want to boost your business by writing a book is merely a fleeting, forgettable thought. It is easy to lose that thought once you get caught up in the whirlwind of little tasks that need to be done. Write your purpose down on a piece of paper. Don't write it as though you are simply wishing for it. Saying "I would like to improve my business by writing a book," is not as powerful as writing it down in the present tense, "My book generates leads for my business and improves my profits by 100%."

Now, put that paper up where you can see it everywhere. Create multiple copies and post one on your bathroom mirror, your kitchen counter, your office desk and just about every place you go to. This will remind your brain what you are up to. Do not discount this as useless self-improvement drivel. Your conscious mind will most likely get tired of seeing your goal statement all the time. However, your subconscious mind thrives on repetition. The more your subconscious mind gets exposed to your written goals, the more it finds ways to work towards it.

Action Steps: Four Easy Steps to Decide Your Book's Purpose

1. Ask yourself: What is the one thing I would like to happen after I write and publish my book? Be clear and specific about what you want and make sure you really want it. Here are some quick thoughts for inspiration.

- You want to make money from your book.
- You want to build or improve your brand.
- You want to increase your visibility.
- You want to improve website traffic.
- You want to stand out from your competition.
- You want to market your business.
- You want to help other people.

2. Take that desire and turn it into a purpose. Do not simply say that you would like to earn money, boost credibility or improve your business. Say that you *will* earn money, boost credibility or improve your business. Be decisive. Own your goal.

3. Write down your purpose and put it up where you will always see it. You can even put it in several places around the house so your subconscious mind will be constantly reminded of it.

3

What's the Big Idea?

A System for Choosing a Book Topic that Sells

"The Author: A person who spends most of their time alone for the purpose of communicating to people."

What will you write about? You now have a goal in mind and on paper. The next thing you need to have before you can blaze a trail to publication is something to write about. Choosing a topic is easy, right? Well, believe it or not, most people get stuck in the book writing process this early. Honestly, we wouldn't dedicate this entire chapter to choosing a book topic if it was that easy.

The most common mistake writers make when picking a topic is deciding on which one they think is most interesting to them. They write only about their thoughts, their beliefs and their passions. That is all well and good if your purpose is simply to exercise your right to free speech. However, when your purpose is beyond expressing yourself in the form of the written word, such as when you want to create a passive income stream or strengthen a business brand, putting your interests ahead of others can be the most damaging thing you can do. Isn't it ironic that you have to put yourself last when you are trying to achieve a business-oriented purpose?

Most amateur authors miss the part where they don't write for themselves. They write for their readers.

It is counter to your goals to choose a topic that sounds good only to you. Instead, it's more important to pick one that sounds good to the people who will read your book. It doesn't mean you should be willing to write about things that bore you to death. It means you should be open to considering other people's points-of-view when you are in the decision-making process.

The Four Questions You Need to Answer Before Deciding on a Topic

There are four factors that determine if a topic is going to unfold into a good book or not: specificity, originality, usefulness and your interest in the topic. When a topic comes to mind and you think there is a possibility that you can write a book about it, run it through these four factors. Does your topic match up to these criteria? If it doesn't, fine-tune it until it meets all four of them, or change your topic altogether.

1. Is it specific enough?

Can you write just one book on something as broad as exercise, social media or cars? You can't. You'll be biting off more than you can chew trying to write a book that covers all the aspects of one sweeping idea. Before you know it, you'll end up spitting out the excess. Besides, people are more willing to spend their money on a book that specifically addresses their pains or improves their lives. If your book, for instance, offers a particular promise to help people increase their website traffic by 300% using a 21-day Facebook marketing program, it is more likely to sell. This is because it gives the reader a good reason to act now compared to a book that gives a vague promise to drive more traffic to their website. It is very specific about what it will do for the reader, how it will be done and when the reader will see results.

However, if you are hell-bent on writing about a broader topic, consider breaking it down into smaller portions to make a series of books. This could be more profitable for you in the end, especially if each book is written on a topic that is distinct and digestible. Readers are too busy to absorb a large chunk of information in one piece. They prefer it served in bite-sized morsels they can easily understand and quickly apply in their own lives.

Perhaps this is the right time to share one experience Al had about writing his first book, *Cheeseburger Abs: Eat What You Want and Look Absolutely Fabulous.* Here is Al taking the floor:

When Nick interviewed Cathy Presland for Writers Rise, I couldn't help but sport a guilty smile. She discussed a common mistake many first-time authors make. She mentioned that they can sometimes be so intent on proving that they are an authority that they include all kinds of information on a wide range of ideas. They don't concentrate on answering one specific question or solving one specific problem. They don't dig deep enough to address one specific concern. Instead, they write on a broad range of topics to show the reader that they know what they're talking about, that they're truly an authority in their field.

That is exactly the trap I fell into when I wrote *Cheeseburger Abs.* Now, I still love that book. I consider it my own personal masterpiece. But frankly, looking back, it is too broad in a lot of different areas. My next book in the *Cheeseburger Fitness* line of books will discuss one specific topic and will solve it thoroughly. This decision was based upon reader feedback and discussing my first book's content with as many people as possible. If I had known this piece of advice then, I would not have made this mistake. But then again, I wouldn't have learned anything new. Once again, we always strive to better ourselves.

2. How original is it?

People say there are no completely original ideas. So how are you going to write about a topic in an original way? Let's take a look at the iPhone. The iPhone is considered one of the biggest breakthroughs in mobile communications. However, the iPhone wasn't a completely original idea. Apple went ahead and took apart its competitors' phones. They picked out the most remarkable features of each phone then combined all features to figure out what was missing. When Apple

> *The most common mistake writers make early on during the book writing process is deciding on a topic that is interesting to them but not to their readers.*

found out nobody had yet come up with a smartphone that had a sleek but easy-to-use interface, they jumped on the opportunity to make their own. And now, we have the iPhone, which sets the bar for other smartphone makers.

In the same way, much of what you do as a writer is take apart all the previous ideas you or other people have come up with and put them together to see if you can work out a gap that no author has ever tried to fill before. It is your responsibility to find that new angle from which you are going to tackle your topic. You have to give your readers a fresh, new way to look at it. For example, the weight loss industry is chock-full of books on losing weight. How do you expect to match up to a competition so massive? In the next page, we talk about a couple of things you can do to create a fresh, unique twist to your book.

 * Incorporate your own story. After all, the most unique thing about your book is that you are writing it, not anybody else. If you have struggled with emotional problems because of your inability to lose weight, for example, or if you found a certain nutrient that was extremely helpful in your weight loss program, build your weight loss book around that.

 * Look for holes and patch them. Not everything that has been said will always be true. Not all theories are backed by hard, cold evidence. In your research, you will probably come up with a few commonly-accepted ideas that you will not agree with. Dispute a

commonly-held belief if you can. If you can't, offer a fresh, innovative approach to a problem that has been always there.

3.   Does it satisfy a need?

People buy non-fiction books for one reason: to gain knowledge. They use this knowledge to satisfy a need that has proven difficult to satisfy. In an authors' convention dinner in Toronto, I (Al here) was fortunate enough to have shared a meal with Dr. John Gray, author of the very popular *Mars and Venus* series of relationship books. Between sips of red wine, he shared with me how important it was to serve your readers' needs first and foremost. You can do this by writing a book first then continue serving their needs with the help of your website.

A lot of people need to know how to date the partner of their dreams. They'd like to know how to lose 10 inches off their waist, deal with their passive-aggressive teenage daughters or learn Emotional Freedom Techniques for self-improvement. These are things that a lot of people need to know more about so they can improve their lives. What do your readers need to know about? You don't have to be a genius to find out what people need. If you already have a blog and have established a following for yourself, ask your readers what they need and want to know more about. People will tell you because they're hoping you can give it to them. If you don't have a blog yet, you can visit online forums and blogs that are related to your topic and look at the kinds of questions people ask. You can then take it from there and attempt to answer these questions in a more in-depth manner.

4.   What makes you excited?

It is not advisable to put your own interests first, but it is also not advisable to put them last. Why? Imagine having to read up on and write about something that you really couldn't care less about. It would be like high school all over again, when you had to write those papers you would rather not. Only it's worse because you're putting yourself through all of it on your own accord. But if you write about something you are passionate about, the journey will be rewarding regardless of how many copies you sell.

When your heart jumps at the slightest thought of your topic and you cannot stop poring over every reading material related to it, you won't need an extra four years in school just trying to learn the things you want to write about. You don't need to have a Ph.D. in psychology to write a book about attracting the right kind of friends and keeping them. If you are happy with your friends and have many of them, you can certainly write a book to teach people how to find the friends they want and build solid relationships with them. Knowledge of a topic doesn't mean you need to have a few letters attached to the end of your name.

At this point, it should already be obvious that "What do you want to say?" is not as crucial a question as "What do your readers want to hear?" Writing a book is no longer about expressing your own thoughts, ideas and opinions. It is about what you want to do to help your readers. This isn't simply so that you can write a book that makes a lot of money, although that's one huge bonus you certainly won't want to turn down. It is more about sharing information other people can use to make their lives better. Doesn't it feel good to know that the words you've written down on paper are improving lives?

Action Steps: An Easy System for Choosing a Book Topic

1. Think about a topic that makes you excited. When you're interested in something, it's impossible not to have any knowledge to write about it.

2. Answer the following questions:

• Is that topic specific?

• Is it original?

• Does it solve a problem?

3. If you answered yes to all three questions, you've got a winning topic. Go for it.

4

You Have Readers Crazy about You

—You Just Don't Know It Yet

"Your website is about you, perhaps that is why you're not getting any traffic."

Know your readers. It's an old writer's adage that has been repeated over and over again. And while every writer has been told time and time again that knowing who you're writing for is one of the most critical aspects of writing a book, be it fiction or non-fiction, not everyone has taken this advice to heart. Maybe it's because you've heard it so many times that it is simply too worn-out to make the right impact. Or maybe you think that being able to throw out an age range, a particular occupation or any one of the two sexes is enough.

You might have come across other people who, when asked about their audience, make half-hearted attempts at telling you they know more than they actually do. For instance, they'd tell you, "My readers are mothers," or, "They are in their 20s and they come fresh from college." The worst we have heard is: "I don't have a specific kind of reader. This book addresses a universal problem. It's for everybody."

Sorry to rain on your parade but no such book is a universal book. It may provide a solution to a problem that all human beings have, but not everybody will want to use your solution. Not everybody will want to read something written with your particular style of writing. For instance, you can write about finding the ideal romantic partner but there are so many ways to approach the topic. How different is a dating book for women in their late 20s and early 30s compared to another dating book written for men in the same age range? Completely and utterly different. And when you're writing for single moms, baby boomers and teenagers, those are still three different books altogether.

The difference lies not just in the writing style. It is also about how you can provide content that deeply resonates with your readers. Let's say, for example, that you're in the party-planning business. You want to write a book that teaches mothers how to plan their child's first birthday party. Now, knowing that your readers are mothers is not enough. You need to understand so much more about these mothers before you can write a book they can align with. How much time do they have on their hands? Does their socio-economic status affect how much they can afford for throwing a party? Are they taxed from having to work all day to come home to a family that needs taking care of? If so, is there a way for you to make sure that your party-planning book won't add more stress to your readers' lives?

These are the things you need to know about your readers. Look beyond who they are on a shallow level. Do your research to understand how they actually live their lives. This is not so you can dictate to your readers who they are or flaunt your knowledge about them. This is so you know how to approach them in the best possible way that appeals to them.

How to Identify Your Readers and Get Under Their Skin

If there is only one thing you need to get right, it is knowing who your readers really are. Some writers may find it useful to think of one ideal reader and even come up with a name for him. It's part of the creative process. They create a life for the reader, make a name for him, hatch up his dreams, motivations and fears and decide his goals in life. In this way, the author is able to reach out to those readers who are very similar to their ideal reader. It isn't always necessary to make up a name for your readers. If it helps, there is no reason why you shouldn't do it. What is important, however, is you know who your readers are well beyond their demographics. The following will help you gain a more solid understanding of your readers and, hopefully, picture them in your mind's eye.

1. Put yourself in your readers' shoes.

A writer's ability to empathize with his readers is gold. A reader will see your book for what it is, not for the masterpiece you might think it is. He will know the value—or lack of—that your book brings to the table. When you can put yourself in the place of your reader and see your book from his perspective, you can easily identify the parts and sections that need reworking if necessary. Don't be afraid to put yourself in the shoes of your reader and ask the crucial questions. What's in it for me if I buy this book? Will it make my life better? If so, how? What will I lose and what will I gain if I buy this book and read it? Knowing the answers to these questions is a good start to crafting a book that is written exactly for your readers.

2. Understand their problems.

When you know that your readers are businesswomen, fast-food restaurant workers or recruitment specialists, do you really know who they are? No, you only know what they do for a living. Doing so is an important first step to understanding your readers. When you know what they do most of their waking lives, you get a general idea of how life is typically like for them.

However, what is more important than knowing their occupations is knowing the challenges they encounter every day. What is their financial situation? Can they afford the solutions you offer? What pressures do they constantly live up to at work? Where are they in the social and political ladder of the organization? These problems go beyond what they encounter at work.

If you are writing a book that involves more personal issues, such as a self-development book on setting goals and achieving them, it is important that you look at all other aspects of your readers' lives. Identify the most common problems that burden them. What are their fears, insecurities and troubles? What are the things they wish for but cannot attain due to one reason or another? What are their dreams, hopes and goals? Knowing your readers' triggers allows you to address issues in ways they can identify with.

3.   Find out what else they read.

If people are truly genuinely interested in a topic, they don't stop at reading one book about it. They realize there is a lot to know about that topic. And so they ask questions. They search blogs. They read more books. They try to find people who share their enthusiasm for the topic and interact with them. These are your competitors, and it's not always a bad thing to have them. In fact, they can actually help you write a better book.

When you know who your competitors are, you gain profound insight into exactly what your readers are looking for. You have a clear idea of the kind of content people are reading. You also learn what forms readers prefer them in. Do they read more books than blogs? Do they prefer watching videos over reading? Checking out your competition is not stealing away their information products. It only means that you are taking advantage of a smart way to understand the kinds of content your readers are looking for.

4.   Don't try to please everybody.

There are more than seven billion ways your book can be interpreted. How do we know this? Well, as of latest count, there are more than seven billion people on this planet. Each of them looks at your book through his own individual filters. These filters were put there by their

Don't try to please everybody. You can't anyway. Work on offering the best you can to your target readers instead.

experiences, peers, parents, teachers, the books they read, the TV shows they watch and so much more. You have your own opinion too. Some people will agree with you and some vehemently won't. This is perfectly okay. That people don't share your opinion on certain issues does not mean you are wrong, or that they are wrong. It only means you have different opinions and that these people will most certainly not want to read your book, much less spend money for it. It's really no problem. The problem only happens when you get all wishy-washy by trying to make everybody on both sides of the argument happy. You won't, and you'll only end up with less people on your side

5.   Picture yourself in a coffee shop.

If you're still having difficulty identifying your readers, try using this technique. Close your eyes and imagine that you're sitting in a coffee shop. Sitting across from you is your ideal reader. Instead of thinking that you are an author and she is your reader, imagine that the two of you are old friends catching up on each other's lives over a cup of coffee. You're sitting back and comfortable. You're enjoying the time spent with your friend at the coffee shop. Now, who is she? What does your friend look like? Is she dressed in a laid-back, down-to-earth manner? How does she talk and sound like? What do you talk about? Does she have any mannerisms or quirks that you can notice? John Steinbeck said he always imagined talking to his aunt, but you can imagine a completely imaginary friend if you like. Once you identify who this friend is, write your book as though you are writing a letter addressed to her.

Action Steps: How to Choose and Understand Your Readers

1. Imagine that you are one of your readers and try to view life from their perspective.

2. Identify your readers' problems and see yourself as having these problems as well.

• How does it feel to experience these problems?

- How would you go about attempting to solve these problems yourself?

- What kinds of solutions do you think will work best for you?

Tip! Do not try to make everybody happy.

Tip! Use the coffee shop technique if you're having problems identifying your reader.

RESEARCH
PHASE

5

Crack Down on Your Competition

The Right Way to Do Research

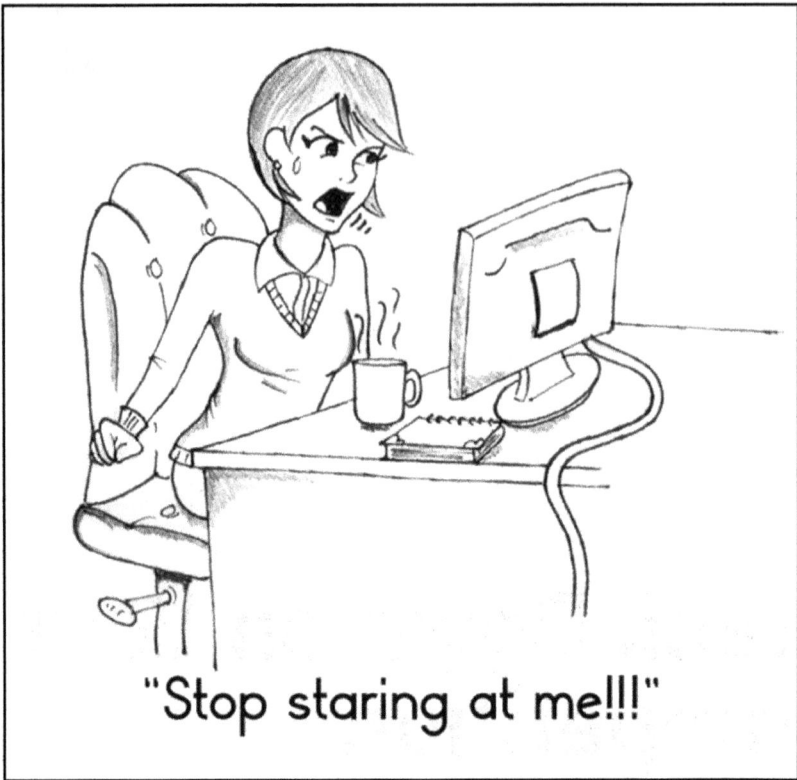

"Stop staring at me!!!"

Arguably, there may no longer be original ideas. Still, there are a lot of original books—and these are the books that sell well. People want something new. They are not looking for another rehash of the same old stuff they have been reading for years. This is why you have to know what has already been written in the past. You don't want to offer your readers something they have already seen.

Is your book the only book of its kind? If you said yes, you must be delusional. Or at least, you haven't done your research on the competition yet. If there are no other books in the same niche as yours, it's very likely that the niche you chose doesn't sell very well. Other writers don't bother going into that field because nobody is buying books about that topic. Fortunately, there are always books written in most niches, no matter how obscure or specific some niches are. However, there is the very rare occasion when you might not be able to find a single book on your topic. If that happens, consider changing your topic altogether.

How to Identify Your Competition in Minutes

Amazon is the best place to start conducting research on your book's competition. It is, indisputably, the biggest marketplace for books and e-books. You can easily go to Amazon to find the books that your readers are looking for. You can also check out other websites that sell books, such as The Nook Book Store by Barnes & Noble, KoBo Books, Apple's iBookstore, Google Play Books, The Sony eBook Store, eBooks.com or your local library.

Amazon, however, is the top-selling site. It doesn't hurt one bit to start your research on Amazon. Looking for books with a similar topic is easy enough. Simply type in the most relevant keyword for your book into the search box at the top of your browser and wait for Amazon to bring in a list of books related to your search.

If your keyword is too general, you will most likely come up with a massive list of thousands of books to look over. That won't do since you don't want to look through each one of those books one at a time. Consider using a more specific keyword. For example, instead of typing "dating and relationships," you could search for "dating for men in their 40s". This will narrow down your search results significantly, making research a lot easier for you. If nothing comes up, browse through the categories for books that are similar to yours. This might take several minutes, but that's a small price to pay for identifying your competition.

On the upper right corner of the results, you will be able to sort the books according to the popularity of the book, prices, customer reviews, ratings and the book's publication date. Choose the "New and Popular" filter to see which books are currently making waves. Make sure you are searching in the Books category so you can use the filter. Also, take a closer look at their average customer reviews and ratings. The more reviews a book has and the higher its star rating, the more likely you're going to get a lot of useful information out of it.

Be extra vigilant when you're looking at star ratings. A book with a 5-star rating doesn't necessarily mean it's better than another book with a 4-star or 4.5 star rating. If the 5-star rating came from one reviewer and the

4-star or 4.5-star book was reviewed by 75 different people, obviously, the 4 or 4.5-star book is more influential because it has reached more people. Therefore, it is more important to look at the popular 4-star book than a not-so-well-known book with top ratings.

Now, even if you've come up with just 10 or 15 books about dating for men in their 40s, that is still an overwhelming pile of books to read. The truth is you don't need to read all of these books. You will need to pick the best books later for research, but you can easily get an idea of how your book will compare to your competition simply by studying the books' descriptions and reader reviews.

It's also a good idea if you can narrow down the initial list so that you'll have a smaller number of books to work on. Use the following criteria to help you figure out which books are worth keeping an eye on and which books can be dismissed.

1. Audience.

The quickest way to trim down your list of competitor books is to find out who the readers of those books are. Let's say you're planning to write the men-in-their-40s dating book. You find a lot of dating books but these are either targeted for middle-aged women or men in their 20s and 30s. Eliminate these books. You will be happy at how much unnecessary clutter you can cut off simply by figuring out who your competitors' readers are.

2. Content.

Different books have different content. That is true even for those who are writing about the same topic and for a similar audience. The most common type of content we see on bestselling non-fiction books is how-to content. How-to is very popular because it guides readers through a practical step-by-step solution. There are also expository books, books that explain a phenomenon in great detail, inspirational books, workbooks filled with exercises and so on. Under which of these categories does your book fall? Now, eliminate all other books that do not belong to the same category.

3.   Depth.

Some books attempt to cover all aspects of a certain topic. Others delve deep into the specific aspects of that same topic. We suggest that you write a book that zeroes in on a specific topic. This makes it easier for you to carve your own place in the book market. Cross out other books that are more of a general overview type of book. Still, it doesn't mean these kinds of books aren't helpful. For example, if all other books are closely focused on different, specific aspects of a bigger topic, you could try to round them all up and create a one-stop guide for readers who don't want to buy all those books.

How to Do Research in Less than Half a Day

The next step after identifying your top competition is to read them. That's part of being hard-core. You have to spend some time and money to buy these books from Amazon and pore over them. You don't have to get everything from Amazon, though. If your friend has a copy of one of those books, go ahead and ask if you can borrow it for a while. Or you can check the local library. And if the local bookstore has a hard copy, it might be better for you to head over there right now so you can start reading in a few hours.

Don't think you can get away with simply reading the reviews. Researching your competition involves so much more than just assessing your position in the market. Much more important is finding all the information you need to pack into your book and create a lot of hard book muscle. In other words, you need to read a lot for you to be able to write a lot.

However, we all have different ways of learning. Some people can absorb a lot of information simply by moving their eyes across the page. Others need to hear the words being spoken out. You can try to read the book out loud if you're planning to end up with a sore throat. But a more convenient way to do this is to head over to iTunes or Audible.com and order an audio copy of the books you bought from Amazon. This way, you can choose which method works best for you, whether you prefer to read the books or listen to the audio books. By now, you should have at least three titles to read or listen to before you begin writing your book. This can be a time-consuming task. Three books is definitely a lot of books to read in a short period of time. Plus, having to absorb three entire books of the same topic can wear you out. This is where we go hard-core. This is where we fast-track the research process so you can absorb as much material as you can in the least amount of time.

In learning theory, the fastest way to absorb information is to have more or even all senses involved. For your research, we suggest that you read the book silently while you listen to the audio book. If you've ever listened to an audio book, you know that the average length is only four to five hours. Now, you don't want to sit four to five hours straight listening to an audio book. You want to speed up the process by adjusting the playback speed 1.5 to two times faster than the normal speed. You can do this with most media players. This change should not be too startling, since most of us can actually comprehend speech that is much faster than a normal audio book. In fact, some research even suggests that your retention increases when you listen at a faster speed because it forces you to pay more attention.

Remember, the goal is to absorb as much information in the shortest amount of time possible. Increasing the speed of your audio book will cut down your listening time to half or almost half of the original four to five hours. Each day, you can set aside just two or three hours to listen to one

The quickest way to learn from these books is to listen to the audio book version while reading along silently with your eyes. Research shows learning is faster when more senses are involved.

audio book. That is only a total of three hours in three days or nine whole hours to practically complete your book research.

However, it is important that you listen actively to what is being said. Active listening means listening attentively. It involves restating, questioning and synthesizing what you are hearing. As you silently follow the words on the book with your eyes, take notes on the margins and white spaces when you need to. Highlight every interesting piece of information you will want to go back to when you finish listening.

Also, have a notebook or a logbook nearby and jot down important questions that you want to ask experts when you interview them later on. We'll talk more about interviewing in a couple of chapters. If it's a library book or a book borrowed from your friend, though, you might want to keep it clean and ink-free and write your notes on a notebook instead.

A Simple Technique to Help You Bolster Your Newfound Knowledge

After each chapter, pause the audio book and create a quick mind map of what you learned. A mind map is a visual representation of a concept or a set of concepts. You can use free and simple mind-mapping software such as XMind or FreeMind. Or you can use good old paper and colored pens.

At the center of the map, write down the central concept of each chapter in three words or less. Then encircle it. From here, draw several lines that branch out from the chapter's main concept. These lines stand for the sub-concepts that support your main concept. Use keywords and key phrases to represent concepts and sub-concepts. Our brains can quickly and easily understand ideas even when they are presented as single words or phrases as opposed to longer sentences. For each sub-concept, draw several little branches where you can write down the details of each idea. Again, use single words and short phrases.

If you are using colored pens, use a different color for each branch or sub-concept. This helps your brain see quickly which ideas belong together. When you have written down all the ideas in one chapter, use the different colored pens to draw boundaries for each idea to make it even easier to recognize them. This technique will help you organize your thoughts about what you read and remember as much information as you can.

Action Steps: How to Pack on Book Muscle

1. Go to Amazon.com and look for books with the same topic as yours. You can also check out other platforms, such as iTunes, the Nook Book Store, eBooks.com, iBookstore, The Sony eReader Store and Kobo Books.

2. Filter out the books that have a different audience from yours, offer different content and have little depth. You should have at least three books remaining. Find out where you can get a copy of these books and get them.

3. Go to iTunes or Audible.com and purchase the audio book versions of the books you got from Amazon.

4. Read at least one book every day while simultaneously listening to the audio book.

5. Create a mind map of each chapter as you go.

6

Secrets from Cyberspace

How to Uncover Priceless
Information from the World's
Most Underrated Sources

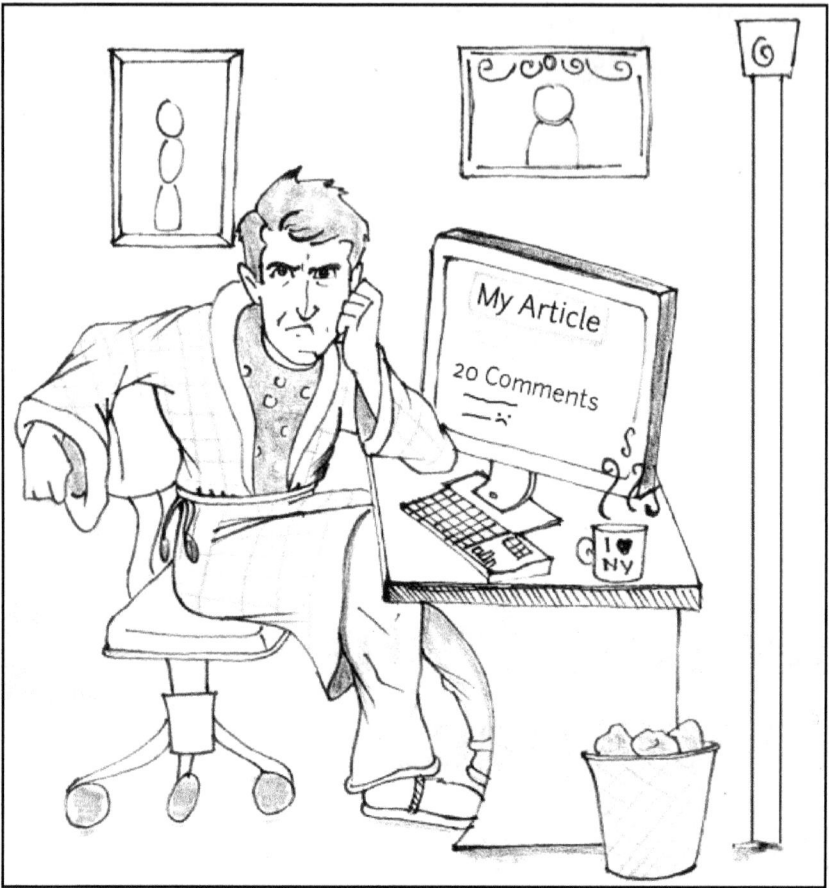

There's something a lot of successful authors don't want you to know. They begin their research with books but they don't end there. Books are awesome sources of information but they are not the only source. Have you ever thought of doing your research online? Some of you might think, "Pfft! That's for lazy people. Why would I want to do my research on the Internet?" But hear us out.

Blogs are your best source of information online. Nobody used to think blogs were credible sources of information. You would expect that with millions of blogs popping up from all over the world, publishing snippets of information that might or might not be true. But the best blogs are actually a gold mine of information. Times have changed. A lot of bloggers have realized they cannot just write and publish whatever they want to gain a loyal following of readers. They have to establish themselves in their chosen fields. They have to meet credibility expectations. And they have found various ways to do that. Of course, there still are blogs out there that publish rubbish. To tell you the truth, there are actually more blogs out there that don't contribute a single good thing to the Internet at all. However, there is no lack of blogs owned and maintained by people who are highly knowledgeable in their fields. This is what makes them highly credible sources of excellent information.

Why You Should Trust Blogs

A public relations firm called Edelman has been publishing a yearly study called the *Edelman Trust Barometer*. The aim of this study is to find out who is most trusted by the general public. In its 2013 edition, Edelman revealed who the top three sources of information are: And so, without further ado, we reveal to you the top three most trusted sources of information. They are the following:

1. Experts or academics (69% trust rating)

2. Technical experts working for a company (67% trust rating)

3. Persons like you (61% trust rating)

So where do bloggers fall into the equation? If you ask us, bloggers fall into the first category, the second category and the third category. They are everything you're looking for all rolled into one.

Bloggers are not experts by virtue of their blogging. If that were true, then even the two-week blogger who never got around to updating his blog after the first two weeks could be called an expert. Bloggers are experts by virtue of all the hard work they put into gathering information and putting it all together in a presentable way for their readers. The best blog owners go through a lot to find the most interesting and relevant piece of information they can offer in a single blog post. And it doesn't end there. For blogs to be frequented by their visitors, bloggers have to regularly dig up their internal and external resources for original content they can publish every week or twice a week.

Additionally, it's an interactive process for them. Unlike book authors, who don't have the opportunity to receive feedback directly from their readers, bloggers continuously learn about their chosen niches by interacting with their readers, answering their questions and getting exposed to alternative viewpoints about their posts. Taking into account the years of research they have done to build an information-rich blog and the continuous learning they go through by regularly interacting with readers, it definitely is no question that bloggers are considered knowledgeable and credible experts in their field.

But bloggers are not just experts. They are people who are just like you and me. If you take a look at how they started, you'll find that most bloggers didn't have the credentials that people traditionally look for in experts. Most of them don't hold Ph.D.s in their field. They haven't gone to school to learn about what they're writing about. But make no mistake about it, the best bloggers have gone through years of self-education and learning on their own. Ask them any question about their field and they will be able to fire back with an informed and insightful answer.

In a lot of ways, you are just like that blogger. You know you have something to share. You know you have an important piece of knowledge that you would like to tell the world. But you don't have the certificate to back up your claims. Just like the blogger first starting out, you're probably struggling to figure out how you can put yourself across as an expert in your field so that people will trust you and buy your book. You probably wouldn't be reading this book if you were pretty confident about writing your own book. But bloggers are people who are just like you. They're regular, simple down-to-earth people who have something important to share. It's okay to trust them.

Three Easy Ways to Find the Best Blogs

Doing your research on other people's blogs is not difficult. Blogs are one of the most accessible and information-rich sources of information you can find on the Internet. Of course, you don't have to read them all. You need to know how to separate the blogs that offer you the most value from those that offer little to none at all. That, too, is not much of a challenge, even for those people who don't make blog-reading a daily habit. If you generally know how to get around the Internet, you will be going through the best blogs about your topic in no time.

1. Search in Google.

A quick and easy way to search for blogs is to do so in Google. Simply search for a keyword that pertains to your topic and attach "blogs" to the end. For example, you can search for "cat grooming blogs," or "fiction writing blogs" or "Mexican cooking blogs." Google Blog Search is even more helpful because it brings you search results that only consist of blog pages. You just have to remove the word "blogs" at the end of your search query. If you're searching for information about cat grooming, for example, Google will bring you blog pages that contain the information you're looking for. You can then check out these blogs to see if they offer more than the initial article that appeared in Google Blog Search.

2. Look in blog directories.

Technorati used to be the end all and be all of blog directories. However, it has become more of an advertising network than an objective directory. Still, Technorati, which has a huge database of blogs in different niches, offers good information about blogs. It indexes 1.5 million blog posts in real-time and updates its overall list of Top 100 blogs and Top 10 blogs in various niches every day.

Several directories have been established as legitimate competitors as well. If Technorati does not offer what you are looking for, you can look at Alltop, Best of the Web Blog Search and Bloggeries.

3. Use blog search engines.

Google may be the king of all searches but you might more easily find the blogs you need by looking in blog search engines. Two important players in blog search are BlogDigger and RSS Feed Search Engine. These websites have a massive collection of RSS feeds of blogs from all over the Internet. When you search an RSS feed on a certain topic, the search engine returns all results pertaining to your search. You can then continue to evaluate the blog connected to each RSS feed and decide whether or not you want to subscribe to that feed.

4.   Go to Delicious.com.

There are massive amounts of information on Delicious.com. You can easily search for top blogs by finding out which posts get tagged the most. Delicious aggregates the most popular web pages on the Internet. These are chosen by people who have seen them. When you have at least one blog you'd like to check out, you can ask Delicious to tell you how many people have tagged the blog's URL. A tag cloud will appear on the upper right of the page. The biggest tag stands for the most number of tags. Click this tag and Delicious will show you several other blogs that are related to your topic.

Using all of these methods or a combination of two or three will quickly help you find several blogs for your research. Three blogs should be a good number to start with. It is okay if you want to read more than that. If you're pressed for time, three high-quality blogs should be able to give you more than enough material to massage and work into your book.

Harnessing the Power of Blogs to Your Favor

There is also the matter of which blog posts you need to read. If you have the time, you can read all of the blog posts written since the beginning of the blog. However, that's not the way we want to work. Who honestly has the time to read everything in a blog that's been set up in 2008? Besides, some of the articles are dated by now. You have to pick out which blog posts will be most helpful to you. Here are a number of ways how.

• Read everything written in the last 60 days.

It is important that you get the most updated information about your topic. Make sure you read through all the latest articles. A high-quality blog usually publishes one to two blog posts every week. That's about only eight to 16 blog posts per blog you need to read.

• Check out the blog's Most Popular Articles.

Somewhere on the sidebar, the blogger usually features the all-time most popular articles on his blog. These articles are usually the most read, most visited and most discussed. There's a reason these articles are popular. It's because they provide useful and interesting information to the readers. This is the kind of information you want to offer to your readers as well.

• Check their stats.

When you're browsing through the titles, you will usually see how many people have shared the blog post on Twitter, liked it on Facebook or gave it a +1 on Google. You will also see the number of comments next to the social media figures. These numbers are an indication of the post's popularity. The higher the numbers, the more likely you're going to get something good out of the blog post.

• Read the comments.

This is one more advantage you can gain from reading blogs but not from reading books. You can get tidbits of input from people who are not bloggers but have a piece of information to share. You will find questions, objections and all kinds of reactions in the comments section. These are usually the same questions, objections and reactions that your readers will have as well. When you know what these are, you are one step ahead of your competition.

Find out how many likes, shares and comments a blog post has. The more likes, shares and comments, the more likely the post is going to be useful for your research.

• Keep an eye out for tips, tricks and techniques.

Bloggers are a creative bunch. Reading their work will most likely help you find several different angles from which you can approach your topic, as opposed to what has been already offered in the books. They also provide a lot of practical, real-world ideas that are quick, easy, no-fuss solutions to our little day-to-day problems. Keep your eye out for these kinds of things.

Do Online Research Offline

Don't attempt to do all your reading online. The best blogs will most likely always be there. However, it is very helpful if you print everything out, including the comments section, so that you have access to your research materials even when you are away from your computer. Having the blog posts printed out on paper also gives you a lot of room for note-taking and highlighting certain concepts. This time, you won't have access to an audio version of each blog post. You won't need that, though, because blogs are way shorter than books.

As always, keep your notebook or logbook ready so you can write down questions that might come up. These questions can be the jump-off point for additional research. You can also add these to a list you can ask experts when you interview them. When you've finished reading one blog post, take out a piece of paper and your colored pens and draw a mind map of what you just read. Just like with your book research, mind mapping will help you reinforce the ideas you have absorbed while reading the blog posts. This will also help you organize the information into a visual diagram that will let you understand the concepts presented in the blog and the relationships between and among them in a faster, easier way.

Action Steps: A Four-Step Approach to Take Advantage of Blogs for Research

1. Look for information-rich blogs dedicated to your topic. There are a number of ways to do this.

- You can look for "(name of topic) blogs" in Google or you can do a more specialized search for your topic in Google Blog Search.

- Check out the top-ranking blogs on Technorati, the most popular blog directory on the Internet. You can also use other blog directories, such as Alltop, Best of the Web Blog Search and Bloggeries.

- Go to blog search engines such as BlogDigger and RSS Search Feed.

- Look for popular posts in Delicious and check out the blogs on which they were posted.

2. For each blog, compile all articles written in the last 60 days. Print them out and read them. Write down your notes and questions. Then create a mind map of each blog post after reading.

3. Look for the most popular articles in each blog. You can do this by checking out the Most Popular list usually featured on the blog's sidebar. You can also look for posts that have the most number of social media likes and shares. If the social media numbers are not posted, look for the articles with the most number of comments.

4. Print out all of these blog posts and read them. Do the same thing as you had done with the first set of blog posts.

7

Lightning-Fast Credibility

The One Thing You Can Do to Make People Believe In You Right Away (And It's Not About Getting a Ph.D.)

When you're writing a book and you have no credentials except an extensive knowledge of the topic you're writing about, it can seem like an impossible feat. After all, why should people believe in someone they don't know? You have to establish credibility. But how do you do that? You can't afford to go back to school to get a certificate in a course that teaches you what you already know, nor can you spend three years building a blog to establish yourself as an expert.

Going hard-core means you have to look beyond the conventional solutions and start getting creative. You may not have time to earn credibility the Ph.D. way, but you can certainly borrow credibility from other trusted sources. But what does it mean to borrow credibility? It simply means to use other people's clout, knowledge and resources to improve your own.

The Secret to Creating Instant Credibility

Let's take a look at it this way. Suppose you find Mark Zuckerberg's ideas on social networking revolutionary. You will probably quote a number of his most notable statements in your book. That is one way to borrow credibility from a prominent person. But it still doesn't quite get you enough credibility to become a trusted source.

What if you did more than lift a Mark Zuckerberg quote off a techno blog? Suppose you were lucky enough to land an interview with him. Mark Zuckerberg himself, founder of the biggest social networking site in the world, flying in to grant you an exclusive interview. That would do so much more than what several of his old quotes can for your credibility. People will start to see you in a new light just because Mark Zuckerberg thinks you're important enough to be given more than the time of day.

However, there's still one big, unanswered question. What if the Mark Zuckerberg types don't have time to give you an interview? Truth be told, they probably don't. They are too busy running their billion-dollar ventures to give practically unknown interviewers the time of day. Even popular mainstream journalists and book authors who have already made a name for themselves and enjoy their fair share of influence still struggle with securing an appointment with them.

That said, there is still no harm in trying to go after the prominent Zuckerberg types. If you score an interview, congratulations! You then have to make sure you are 100% prepared to tackle the interview with an industry giant. But if you don't get the interview, don't be too hard on yourself. There are several other people who can grant you an interview to help you boost your credibility and increase the value of your book at the same time.

Have you ever thought of Jack Dorsey? Jack Dorsey is not as well-known in popular media as Mark Zuckerberg. Maybe it's because he doesn't figure in a lot of controversial news stories as the latter does. But being one of the three co-founders of Twitter makes him just as credible as Mark Zuckerberg himself. It's the types like Jack Dorsey who like to keep a low profile that just might be happy and willing to give you an interview. You just have to be open enough to approach people you have initially never heard of.

And even if Jack Dorsey does not accept your invitation for an interview, don't fret. Settling for less prominent people does not mean you're not as hard-core as you'd like to believe. Consider going after the people that Mark Zuckerberg and Jack Dorsey trust. They most likely have multitudes of assistants, colleagues and friends who are very credible sources of information and can add more value to your own book. These are the people that Mark Zuckerberg or Jack Dorsey would endorse. It is worth taking the time to go after them when the people like Mark Zuckerberg and Jack Dorsey are not available.

A Quick Way to Find an Expert to Interview

Ideally, the best people to interview are those who are famous in their fields. But if they don't have the time to speak with you, go for their assistants and friends. The people who report to them day in and day out or the people they would meet at a coffee shop for a chat over a few cups of coffee are the people who are not as well-known but still possess the right knowledge and experience to answer your questions.

But what if you're nowhere near this network of people? What if you can't get Mark Zuckerberg to give you an interview? What if you have no idea how to reach out to or even find one of his friends or colleagues to interview?

Your goal is not to find the flashiest, most prestigious names to add to your book. Your goal is to find people who have established themselves as experts in their fields of specialization. Remember the *Edelman Trust Barometer*? People trust technical experts and academics. They also trust people who are just like them. Mark Zuckerberg may be a technical expert, but he certainly isn't like the regular guys you see walking down the street every day.

For example, do the names Francisco Rosales and Jeff Bullas sound familiar? People who don't have a passion for social media marketing may shake their heads and say no. But if you're writing a book about social media, you're writing a book for people who are interested in social media. You have a specific, targeted reader who can greatly appreciate the fact that you offer exclusive information from two of the top social media bloggers on the Internet. While the mainstream reader might not have heard of them, your target audience most likely have. That is what really counts. And even if they haven't, just one Google search shows them how much

A Quick Look at the
Other Benefits of Conducting an Interview

Interviews don't simply add to your credibility as a writer. They also add to the knowledge you want to share. They provide new insights from other people and help widen your understanding of the topic. They offer a break for the reader by adding other voices into the discussion. They give your non-fiction a human touch by showing your readers that real people and not just piles of books and papers were involved in the making of your book. When interviews are done right, they can become one of the best sources of information you can use for your book, while building your credibility at the same time.

value they're going to get from your interview. For the targeted reader, one who is looking for a specific piece of information, prominence is not as important as expertise.

The same thing applies to academics. People may not recognize the name Dr. This-and-That, but academics are also experts who gained knowledge through the years. The main difference between academics and bloggers is that the former acquired expertise through formal training. The similarity is that academics, like bloggers, also continuously learn in their fields. Most academics simply don't just teach. They are involved in research and industry projects relating to their field so that they can speak to you from both a theoretical and practical perspective. The good thing about interviewing academics is that there is always at least one in your locality you can approach. You can conduct your interview via email or phone. Or you can meet in person, which allows you to build greater rapport and a deeper relationship with your interviewee.

Al recently had an interview with Loren Christensen, a martial arts veteran and author of 46 books. Can you believe that? The man has written almost 50 books. If you check out his Amazon author's page, you'll see that all of his books have four to five-star ratings. That's just amazing! Now, if your readers have no background in martial arts, this may be their first time to hear the name Loren Christensen. But if they have an interest in martial arts, law enforcement or self-defense, his name will definitely ring a bell. As a side note, we also talk about some of the great stuff Al learned from his interview with Loren. You'll read all about it on the Writers Rise blog.

Now, let's go back to our main topic. Just how many people should you plan to interview? We think you should interview three experts for your book. Three is definitely a lot of people to interview. If you have no experience with interviewing before, interviewing three people can be a very daunting experience. Do not worry, though. The sooner you start interviewing, the easier it will be for you to approach the next person. Aside from that, we will show you exactly what you need to do.

The Best Way to Get Granted an Interview

A lot of interviewers and interviewees agree. The best way to conduct an interview is by meeting in person. Still, this can't always be possible. What if the person you chose to interview lives halfway across the globe?

Thank heavens we now have easy, fast and Internet-based means of communicating with other people. Before you contact a person you want to interview, think first about how you want to interview him. Will it be via phone or by email? Both have their own advantages and disadvantages but you should also consider the preferences of your interviewee.

Interviewing experts in your field won't only add richer information to your research. It will also increase your credibility because you're telling your readers that experts trust you enough to give you an interview.

Cold-calling is not an option. We suggest you start by sending a letter in the mail. We're not talking about email. We're talking about snail mail—letters printed out on paper and have a stamp on them. Use FedEx for delivery so you can track where your letter is and if it has been received. If you're trying to contact a blogger, email is most likely his preferred means of contact. However, for other people who hold prominent positions in their industry, good old-fashioned snail mail is still the way to go. When you know that your letter is received, give the person a call and mention the letter.

Here is where a lot of first-time interviewers make their first big blunder. You might assume that a person will be happy to grant you an interview. After all, wouldn't you be flattered when someone wants to interview you? But instead of assuming someone is honored to be interviewed, turn things around and be honored that you have an expert to interview. That person is doing you a huge favor, so give her a compelling reason to want to be interviewed. You could offer advertising space for his projects in your book. Or you could feature him on your website. Or it could also be the very simple fact that you are a huge fan of his work. Be honest, though. If you say that, you really have to be a big fan. The interviewer will know if you're only trying to flatter him to get that interview.

You can also ask how much it would cost for him to grant you an interview. Most people, even those in positions of high power, will not ask for compensation to be interviewed. However, if your prospect gives you a figure, consider how much informational value and credibility he can lend and decide accordingly.

There Are Only Three Ways to Conduct an Interview

Once your interviewee agrees to be interviewed, ask if she prefers to speak with you in person or via phone or email then take it from there. When she replies, it is best to agree with the mode and schedule she prefers and stick with it. If you're not available during that time, politely inquire about another schedule and see if you can speak with her during that time. As a rule of thumb, it is always better that you go out of your way to make time for the interviewee's first schedule.

If you choose to speak over the phone or through Skype, it will be easier for you to make a connection with your interviewer. You will be speaking to each other face to face instead of sending emoticons over email. You will also most likely finish faster because you can have the conversation in half an hour or so and have all your questions answered right away. However, the biggest advantage of phone interviews over email is that you can quickly fire off follow-up questions right after your interviewee answers your prepared questions.

But email also holds its own merit as a medium for conducting interviews. First of all, you're not being as intrusive as when you're holding phone interviews. You let the interviewee answer your questions in her own time. There are no worries when it comes to picking a schedule that works well for the two of you, which can sometimes be difficult if the interviewer and interviewee live on opposite sides of the world. And lastly, interviewing via email does not require you to record the conversation or type down your scribbled notes into a neater MS Word document. It has already been done for you.

Again, make sure to check with your interviewee the mode she prefers for the interview. After all, she is granting you a huge favor by allowing you to interview her. She is in a position to choose what makes her most comfortable.

Pre-Interview Preps You Shouldn't Miss

Now that you've scored an appointment, it's time to get yourself ready to conduct that interview. People who agree to answer your questions are, to some extent, flattered that you would consider them experts. Therefore, it is your duty as interviewer to live up to their expectations. And to tell you the truth, interviewees have very high expectations of their interviewers.

Do not, in any way, try to fool around while you're gathering their opinion. Preparation before the interview is essential. You can't just walk up to the venue you've agreed upon and expect that you'll simply fire away with your brilliant questions to wow your interviewee. On the contrary, you might even feel terrified at the thought of speaking with someone considered an expert in his field. Lots of people do. We know we did.

It can be nerve-racking to conduct your first interview. You might suddenly think that the questions you have in mind sound sillier and sillier by the minute. You might even get too nervous to pay attention to your interviewee's answers and fail to ask follow-up questions. But if you come prepared with a list of good questions, a voice recorder and something for you to jot down your notes, it definitely helps with the jitters.

Take a look at the following interview preparation tips that will be useful to you when you find an expert to interview.

1.   Research your interviewee.

Look him up on Google. Find out what he has been doing at least in the last couple of years. Nothing can be more frustrating than an interviewer who starts off with questions that could be answered simply by looking at the About page on the interviewee's website. If you're interviewing a blogger, you have a ton of material to work with for your initial research. If he has been blogging since forever, that is, since the beginning of the Internet, then make sure you've gone through all his blog posts in the last two months. If you're pressed for time, at least go through your interviewee's About page and all of his most popular blog posts.

2.   Ask informed questions.

Your initial research will give you quite an obvious picture of who the interviewee is, what he does and what he stands for. Instead of asking the basic questions you're not supposed to ask during the interview because they have already been answered somewhere else, ask the questions with no answers yet.

Shel Israel of *Forbes* gives an example when he was scheduled to interview David Sachs, CEO of Yammer, an enterprise social network for businesses and professionals. At the time of his interview, Sachs had just recently issued a statement that his company will be offering a $25,000 hiring bonus for Yahoo employees. Israel had done his research and saw that other journalists like him had already asked Sachs about this. It wasn't appropriate for Israel to ask the question again since he already knew the answer. So when interview day came, Israel asked

Sachs about the number of resumes he had received after that statement and the number of job offers he had given.

This interview was for a story in a news publication, but Israel's ingenuity in looking for the unpatched holes can definitely be applied when conducting interviews for your book.

3.   Create a focus.

Having a specific topic to talk about helps you create a focus for your interview. There will be instances when your interviewee will wander and veer off to other things he would like to talk about. Remind yourself that you're doing the interview to find out more about a certain topic. This allows you to shift the conversation back to that topic. After all, an hour or two isn't enough for you to talk about the interviewee's thoughts about life in general.

For example, if you were conducting the interview to talk about methods for easing depression with hypnotherapy, craft your questions around that topic. Save the rest for another day, if you're lucky enough to be granted a second or third interview. If you do the first interview well, you most likely will be granted subsequent interviews.

4.   Ask other people.

If you're stuck, you can always rely on other people to create questions for you. If you have a blog and your own loyal following, it might be helpful for you to tell your readers that you're going to interview Mr. So-and-So. If they have any questions for him that they would like to get answered, they can post them in the comments box. Take a look at which questions are headed in the same general direction as your questions, then add them to your list. You can also check out online forums and see what questions people are asking about a certain topic.

5.   Write open-ended questions.

Obviously, you will have to ask a few technical questions that require technical answers, such as: "When did you leave your job to become a full-time Internet entrepreneur?" or "How long have you been coaching business executives?" However, the most interesting questions are always those that give the interviewee a lot of space to be more thoughtful. It is those questions that ask for deeper, more insightful answers. For example, if you have to ask about the last time the interviewee worked at a full-time job, follow up with something more provocative, such as "How different has your life been ever since?" or "Do you have any fears or worries about the lack of security that comes from not having a regular job?"

6. Use your competition's sales letters.

This is a technique taught to us by Jimmy D. Brown and it's a great way to take advantage of your competitors' sales letters to create interesting interview questions. Here is how it works. In every well-written sales letter, there is a list of benefits that people can gain from the product or service.

For example, if you're writing a travel book, then your competitors' sales letter will most likely list the benefits of reading their travel book. One benefit that might be included is readers can score cheap travel packages that are normally available only to agents and not travellers. Now, simply take that benefit and turn it into a question. Instead of buying your competitor's book to get more information, ask your interviewee, "What are some ways people can find cheap travel packages that are normally only available to travel agents?"

11 Rules for Conducting an Interview

The big day has arrived. Armed with your list of questions, a few pep talks and several deep breaths before meeting with your interviewee, you are now ready to take on the big interview. However, there are a few more things you need to remember to conduct a successful interview. In a nutshell, it is all about two things: 1.) giving the interviewee the due respect he or she deserves as an interviewee and 2.) ensuring that you take down every single piece of information that the interviewee gives away. In the next page, we're going to take a more detailed view.

1. Remember that this is not about you as the expert.

You are an expert in your field. You wouldn't be able to even think about writing a book if you are not. But in this interview, you are the one looking for information and the interviewee is the only person who can give you that. It doesn't matter that you are asking very intelligent questions if your interviewee feels uncomfortable. Don't try so hard to impress. Try harder to relate.

2. You control the interview; but, again, it's not about you.

It's about the person you're interviewing. It's about their thoughts on a topic you'd like to know more about. Do let them speak. That is what you're here for, after all. However, keep in mind that you are the interviewer and you still control the flow of the conversation. If the interviewee starts musing about the possibility of extra-terrestrial life on other planets when you specifically asked him to talk about the unemployment rate in North America, you have every right to say, "Very interesting, but you see, I wanted to ask you about this..."

3. Be prepared to listen.

Listening is underrated. No, we don't think you plan to be impolite by ignoring your interviewee's answers because you have a voice recorder anyway. We think that a lot of people get anxious when they're interviewing someone for the first time. They tend to focus on getting rid of their anxiety and tuning out everything else. Trying to stop yourself from feeling anxious is not a bad thing. But when you're interviewing someone, you're losing out on the opportunity to connect, ask follow-up questions and dig up answers you and your interviewee did not even expect to come up. So do your best to really listen.

4. Establish rapport.

This is essential. If you want the interviewee to give you great answers, you have to make him feel comfortable. And that means you have to make him feel that you're there as a friend, not as an enemy ready to attack. To establish rapport, you have to treat the other person with the utmost respect. Treat him like you would treat anybody who is doing you a huge favor, but don't fall on your knees and prostrate yourself at his feet either. Act in a way that shows you deserve the same kind of respect you're giving him. Each of you should have the same positive impressions of each other for the interview to go well. You can achieve this with the use of body language.

The following are a few basic tenets of body language you can use to build better rapport with the other person:

∗ Sit with an open body stance. Keep your legs and arms uncrossed and turn your heart towards the other person's heart.

∗ Look him in the eye but be careful not to overdo it. Looking at another person straight in the eye all the time can make other people uneasy. Aim for around 60% to 70% eye contact. Also, if you're uncomfortable looking someone in the eye, aim for the space between the eyes. The other person will think you're looking at him in the eye when you're really not.

∗ Mirror the other person's body language. Countless studies have shown that subtly matching other people's body language is a great way to make them feel good being with you. If she leans forward, lean forward too. If she tilts her head, tilt your head too. And if she speaks in a soft, slow tone, do the same as well. The keyword here is subtle. If the other person catches you trying to mimic her, it might not work for you.

∗ Smile. Smiling works wonders all the time. The key here is to smile a genuine smile. Most people can identify at a subconscious level which smiles are fake and which ones are real. The proof is in the way your eyes light up when you smile. If your cheeks don't rise and the crinkles around your eyes don't show up, that's when others know you're not smiling for real.

5.   Take notes.

You may have a voice recorder but it won't pick up all the quality information you might need to pick up. For example, if you're interviewing a fashion icon, you might want to take note of her outfit.

> *Smile. Nothing works wonders than smiling a genuine smile, the kind that makes your eyes crinkle and the apples of your cheeks go up.*

That says a lot about her personal style more than her words. Or you can note down other things, such as her facial expression when she answers a particular question, which questions she laughed at before answering or if she looked out the window for a while to think about her answer. These non-verbal signals can clue you in on a lot of things about the interviewee that you would otherwise not get if you simply listened to what she said.

6.   Livescribe's smartpen is a great tool.

We are not saying that you have to go out and buy it, but we think it is a great investment. You can use it for taking notes during interviews and organizing them afterwards. It's simply a digital pen you can use on a special kind of paper and then transfer electronically to Evernote, a note-taking and archiving application. You can also use it to record the audio of interviews, which can also be uploaded to Evernote afterwards.

7.   Make sure any equipment you need is working fine.

This sounds pretty obvious but there are some writers out there who still have to go through the awkward I'm-sorry-but-I-seem-to-be-having-technical-problems stage at the beginning of the interview. If you're using Skype to conduct phone interviews, it pays to invest in a good microphone and headset so that you and your interviewee can hear each other well. Make that test call before each interview because you never know when your computer might start acting up.

And it's not just your computer you have to check. Make sure you have a high-quality voice recorder that will not suddenly stop in the middle of the interview because you ran out of space. The ancient tape recorder is defunct by now, but most smartphones can be installed with apps that allow you to record long interviews and do a variety of things with your recordings. A good app allows you to transfer recordings to your computer, improve the quality of recordings and share them via email or cloud storage.

8.   Send the questions in batches.

If you're interviewing via email, divide your questions into batches. A good rule of thumb is to send five questions first. Then wait for the interviewee to send the answers back before you send the next batch of questions. This way, he won't be overwhelmed by a long list of questions at one time. Of course, it's a good idea to tell your interviewee that you're going to send the questions by group so he can expect another round of questions when he's finished with the first one.

9.   Show that you're listening.

Paraphrasing or summarizing the interviewee's statements is one way to show you're not tuning out. You can say what he just said in your own words and ask if your interpretation is correct. For example, say, "What you're basically telling me is that people can get rich on the Internet, provided they commit a lot of time and hard work to it. Is my interpretation right?"

However, listening well goes beyond listening for the facts. You have to look out for the emotions behind what the interviewee is saying. If he just described for you how he received 65 rejection letters before his first novel got published, you can probably imagine how that feels. Say, "Wow! That must have been harsh!"

10. Keep quiet.

This is an old journalist trick that most book authors don't know about. When an interviewee suddenly stops after a long stream of words, stay quiet. This is not an opportunity to cross off another question on your list and get it over with. These usually five-second bouts of silence are often moments of reflection. The interviewee is figuring out how to put into words all the things he wants to tell you. There are little jewels of insight in those moments. Let the silence be for a while. Allow the interviewee to form an astounding response.

11. Leave with a thanks.

Show your gratitude for the interviewee's time and effort. A word of thanks is fine, but go the extra mile saying thank you by offering a token or a promise to send him your book for free once it gets published. Also, in case the interviewee remembers something he forgot to mention during the interview, it would be good if you left your contact information so that he has a way of contacting you again if he wants to.

Special Bonus Alert!

We want to make interviewing easy for you, so we did what we could do best. We prepared a special file for you that contains up to 202 possible questions you can ask the person you will interview. Simply go to www.HardCoreSoftCover.com to download your special bonus today

Action Steps: Eight Steps to Building Quick Credibility Through Interviews

1. Find at least three experts who are willing to give you an interview. Start by contacting prominent, A-list types like Mark Zuckerberg or Jack Dorsey. You can also go for their assistants, friends and colleagues. Also, reach out to bloggers, academics and other experts in your field.

2. Send each one of them a letter via snail mail, preferably through FedEx. When they receive the letter, give them a call and refer to the letter you sent them. If you're interviewing a blogger, he might prefer to be contacted

through email. Look at his contact page and act accordingly.

3. Offer the person something he cannot resist, such as an advertisement for his business on your book.

4. If he agrees to give you an interview, decide on a time, place and mode of interview. Give priority to the interviewee's preferences.

5. Thoroughly think about your questions and write them down.

6. Get your pen, notebook, recorder and all other equipment ready for the interview.

7. Arrive at the interview early. Establish rapport by being friendly and respectful before jumping into the interview.

8. Ask your questions. Listen well and follow up or summarize.

9. Thank the interviewee for his time. Leave your contact information so he can contact you if he wishes.

8

How to Survive Your Research Hurricane

An All-in-One Solution for
Organizing Your Notes

"Hello this is 911, What is your emergency?"

Even before you begin writing your book, you will have to work with tons of information. You'll be working with information about your book's competition, information about your interviewees and the heaps and piles of information about your topic that you will get from other books, blogs, websites, periodicals, journals and other sources. That's a lot of material to work with. It's easy to get lost in a sea of information if you don't put an effort into organizing all those little pieces of data into a manageable system that can help you create a book.

Each of us has our own ways of organizing. Some people like to sort their notes into neat, little color-coded folders. They can easily pull out the information they need simply by taking a look at the color of the folder. Others use note-taking and organizing software such as Evernote to put their notes together in digital files. Still, others prefer the old-fashioned way of writing down their notes on paper then transferring them to the computer afterwards. The mind-mapping approach we introduced a while back is also a very helpful way for you to understand your notes at a glance.

Some others prefer the haphazard approach. They take down their notes on whatever they could get their hands on, but they don't attempt to sort it out later on. You might prefer this method. We think it makes it a tad bit more difficult to find what you're looking for when you need it, though. Imagine thinking, "What was that cool thing he said about likening friendships to spiders weaving webs again? Come on, come on. Think!" After a while, you realize you've lost your flow of thought. You are now recklessly going through your uncoordinated pile of papers scanning for the word "spiders".

Of course, each person is free to choose how he organizes his research. You can make mind maps. You can use Evernote. Or you can take down notes however you choose to. We strongly suggest you pick out one note-taking and organizing method. There is bound to be one that works for you. Let's talk about these methods in more detail below.

A Simple, Easy System for Taking Notes and Synthesizing Information

In the 1950s, a Cornell University professor named William Pauk devised a note-taking system that he advocated to his students. This system works very well in cases when the students have to synthesize the information they just learned and reinforce their knowledge. Clearly, this note-taking method was made for the classroom. However, there's no reason it shouldn't work well for authors and researchers.

The Cornell method involves dividing the page into two columns. The column on the right should be twice as wide as the column on the left. This is where you will write down your notes on what you have read. After you finish reading and taking notes, write down the important keywords, phrases and questions you might have on the left column. Leave around two inches of empty space at the bottom of each page. This is where you summarize each idea you took down during your research. When you begin to write, it will be easier for you to find the notes you're looking for by flipping through the pages and scanning the left columns for the right keywords and phrases.

Grandma's Index Card Technique

The Index Card Technique is probably older than your grandma. But if it has been around since that time, the only reason is because taking notes using reliable old index cards is still helpful to a lot of researchers.

If you haven't tried this system when you were in school, it goes like this. You take a stack of little 3x5-inch or 5x7-inch index cards and use them to write down your notes about single ideas or quotations. On the upper left corner of the index card, write down the keyword so that it is easy for you to locate that particular note when you need to. On the upper right, you take down the name of the source, the name of the author and, if applicable, the page number where you found that piece of information.

You might need lots and lots of index cards if you're going to use this system, but it will be a whole lot easier for you when you need to look up a detail you need right away. If you really want to be very meticulous, use different colors of index cards for different sub-topics. For example, if you're writing about caring for Labradors, you can use green index cards for notes about feeding, blue for grooming, white for vaccines and so on.

The Magic You Can Do with Evernote

Evernote is a breakthrough in collecting, storing, organizing and retrieving information. It has definitely made life easier for a lot of people who conduct the majority of their research on the Internet. And it also provides a lot of value for those who like to simply browse and read up on a lot of stuff.

You can gather different kinds of online information, including texts, images, web pages, URLs, sound clips and videos. You can then organize them into specific notebooks in Evernote. You can also create text notes, audio notes and webcam notes from scratch. Aside from that, you can also

Use Evernote to collect, store, organize and retrieve all sorts of information you find on the Internet. You can also use Livescribe's smartpens with Evernote.

classify each note into different notebooks that you can create and give custom names. To make retrieving your information easier, you can add tags to identify your note. For example, you can create a note about a smoothie recipe and tag it "smoothie recipes". The next time you're looking for all your smoothie recipes, you can simple choose the tag "smoothie recipes". Evernote will automatically bring back all the relevant notes for you.

Another cool thing about Evernote is that it works particularly well with Livescribe's smartpens. Any handwritten notes or audio recordings you make using the digital pen can be automatically transferred to Evernote in digital form. You can easily access all these notes because you can sync your Evernote account, allowing you to view all your notes whether you're working on your computer, your phone or your tablet.

There are two versions of Evernote: the free version and the premium version. Honestly, we use the free version because it offers such a wide range of functionality that we haven't found a need to upgrade. Before you shell out your hard-earned money on the premium version, try out the free version first.

Action Steps: Five Ways to Take Notes and Organize Your Research

1. Use the Cornell Note-Taking System to help you synthesize your notes. Divide a sheet of paper into two columns. The right column should be three times wider than the left column. The right column is where all your notes go. On the left side are major keywords, ideas and questions about what you've just read. At the bottom of each sheet is a short summary of your notes.

2. Get a bunch of index cards and take separate notes on each of them. Place the keyword on the upper left corner and the details of the source (i.e. name of source, name of author and page number) on the upper right. If you want to be more organized, you can also use different colors of index cards for notes with different topics.

3. Keep track of your notes online using Evernote. Simply create a notebook with the name of your book and put all your notes in there. Or you can create separate notebooks for the research you've done on books, another for research done on blogs and another for interview audios and transcripts.

4. Use Evernote for gathering research on the Internet. It can store and organize text, images, videos, audios and web pages. If you're using a smartpen from Livescribe, you can also use Evernote to store whatever text notes or audio notes you have recorded with your digital pen.

WRITING
PHASE

9

Whip Your Research into Shape

How to Transform Your Notes into an Outline

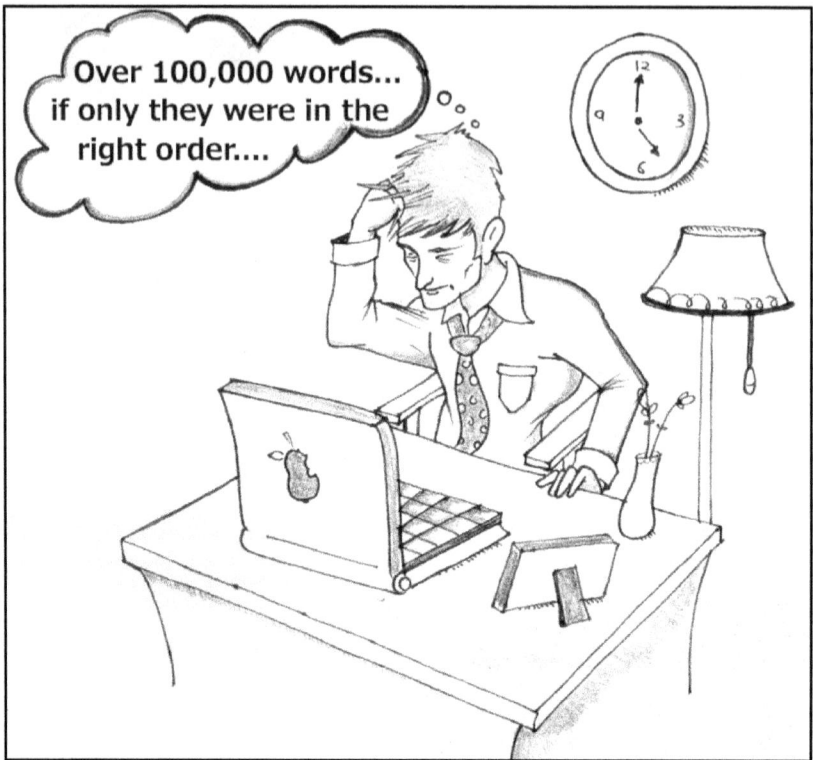

Congratulations! If you've finished the Research Phase, then you're halfway through the book writing journey. You might think it means nothing to be halfway through. You haven't even written a thing yet, after all. But if you have gone through the grueling research stage—read at least three books, three blogs and interviewed at least three people, recognize that this is one big accomplishment. You deserve a pat on the back for it.

Now, you understand what we mean when we said at the beginning of this book that writing a book is more than just sitting down in front of your computer to come up with the paragraphs that make up your first masterpiece.

This chapter marks the beginning of the Writing Phase. This is where you finally get to sit down in front of your computer and hack away at your keyboard. However, you won't be working with putting the sentences and paragraphs that will magically turn into your book just yet. You still have one very important preparatory step to take before you finally get to write. You have to learn how to create an outline first.

What is an Outline and Why is It Important?

Brainstorming can be, well, a stormy process. So is doing your research. That's typical. You can expect that anyone going through the creative process may need to have scattered thoughts, notes and papers before he can put it all together in one neat and orderly pile. However, good writers use one beneficial technique that allows them to sort through the mess and pick out the parts that are going to be most useful and relevant for their book. For a lot of writers, outlining is a priceless tool.

Imagine a teacher who enters the classroom with no real objectives about what to teach the children for the day. Or a construction team that attempts to build a house with no idea of what the final house will look like. A writer who jumps in front of the computer with no outline to guide him through the writing process is just like the teacher and the construction worker who take on a project with no clear and visible idea of the end result. Without an outline to serve as your map of your unwritten book, you will find yourself lost and directionless very soon.

An outline also gives you a visual idea of how much you have to do. The reason many people are petrified at the thought of writing their own book is because the task looks too massive and therefore impossible to do. However, a great way to conquer any seemingly undoable project is to break it down into digestible little chunks that you won't be afraid to take on. Outlining helps you break your book into shorter chapters and sub-chapters. This allows you to see your book writing project as a series of little tasks that can be done one task at a time instead of one big massive slab of responsibility you have to take on all at once.

For example, you can decide that one little task equals writing one chapter. If you commit to doing one task a day, then book writing isn't going to be so hard. Most non-fiction books contain on average somewhere between 1,500 and 5,000 words per chapter. That means you can resolve to write that certain number of words every day until you finish writing the entire length of your book. Of course, those are average figures. You may opt to write less or more than that amount of words. The important thing to remember is that you can manage the writing process more effectively if you break down your book into shorter pieces by creating an outline.

Should You Write an Outline Before or After Research?

Some people ask, "Doesn't it make sense to write an outline first before you do the research?" They've got a point. If you create a rough outline before you hit the books, it is easier for you to identify what is missing. You can take on a more focused approach towards your research this way. However, other people argue that you can't make an outline before you do your research because you don't have the right information to create an outline with. Well, they also have a point.

The thing is an outline should not be seen as a rigid structure you have to strictly follow at all times. Outlines are flexible. They can be adjusted to adapt to what you think your readers need. You don't have to write an outline only once. You can write it and re-write it until you feel you have found the perfect structure for your book.

Writing an initial outline before any research is done allows you to identify your knowledge gaps. It helps you discover the kind of information you need so you can write your book. By doing competitor research, you also ensure that you don't waste your time writing a book that is strikingly similar to what someone else has already written. Instead, your research will help you gain knowledge about your place in the market and what you need to do to stand out from the rest. That's why we recommend doing the research before finishing the outline.

After you've finished your research, you can go back to your initial outline and insert all the new information you have learned in all the most logical places. Or you can create a new and improved outline with the new information you now have from research.

If you have no idea where to begin with the outline, conduct your competitor research first. This will help you gain a general idea of what has already been discussed about your topic. It will also help you formulate your own ideas about the topic and develop an outline based on relevant and updated information you have read during your research. Writing a book requires that you have extensive knowledge about what you're writing about. This means you will have to populate your head with ideas first before you can sit down and create an outline.

Five Quick Steps for Creating a Useful Outline

Contrary to what your high school teacher might have taught you, creating and developing an outline is no difficult task. Since you're not writing for your teachers anymore, it's okay to do away with all the technical niceties. It doesn't matter whether or not you choose to write a sentence outline or a topic outline. It doesn't matter that your categories are written in parallel form to one another. It doesn't even matter that you're using the proper numbering format for your outline. None of that matters.

You can even write your initial outline on a table napkin if you need to, just as long as you transfer it into something a little more permanent later on. What matters is that you can organize your ideas into a logical, understandable form in a way that won't take you days or even hours to comprehend. If you've got a clear idea of your book's big picture, you can create your outline in less than half an hour.

- Step 1: Identify your main topic.

If you already know what you want to write about, it won't take long for you to finish this step. Anyway, by the time you reach this point, you should already know what your main topic is. Just be sure that you're working with a specific, original and useful topic. Have you decided to write a general overview book? Or will you have a more specific focus? Like we said, either of the two works as long as you stick to your decision along the way.

- Step 2: Identify your main categories.

A non-fiction book is typically divided into three parts: the introduction, the body and the conclusion. The introduction and the conclusion normally get their own chapters, but the body forms the bulk of the book. The body is where you discuss the main categories in separate sections. For example, if you're writing about natural acne treatments, the main categories could include the following:

- What is Acne?

- The Major Causes of Acne

- Natural Acne Treatments

• Step 3: Identify your sub-categories.

The sub-categories provide support to the main categories. A good sub-category that can go under the category "What is Acne?" is "Where Acne Comes From" or "The Different Kinds of Acne". Under "The Major Causes of Acne", you can include "Hormonal Causes" and "Myths about Diet and Acne". And under "Natural Acne Treatments", you can organize the sub-categories according to the kind of treatments available, such as "Topical Treatments", "Oral Treatments" and "Homeopathic Treatments".

• Step 4: Identify the supporting topics to your sub-categories.

You can go even deeper into the outline if you need to. Under the sub-category "Topical Treatments", you can still list down the different natural topical acne treatments that you're going to discuss one by one in your book. For instance, you can add "Tea Tree Oil", "Witch Hazel" and "Grapeseed Oil" under this sub-category.

• Step 5: Identify examples, stories and other supporting elements.

By providing your readers with real-life stories and examples, you give them a glimpse of how the information you write about works in our human lives. If you're a witness to the effectiveness of tea tree oil as a natural acne treatment, for example, devote a section in your book to your story about it. A non-fiction book can only come alive with stories like this.

The outline template you can see on the right goes on until you reach the last chapter of your book. It is a basic and typical outline and it works all right with a lot of topics. However, feel free to play around with the order of things if you feel it will help you be more effective in presenting your information. The point of writing an outline is so you can create a path you can follow when you begin writing your book. Remember, you create that path, not anybody else. If the path you have to take is different from the typical path prescribed by your teachers, so be it. Most of life's most remarkable discoveries were made on the paths less travelled.

Also, do not think that once your outline has been set that there is no other way for you to go but to follow it. If, in the middle of writing your

Here is How an Outline
Usually Looks Like

When you're done writing your outline, it will look a lot like this:

I. Introduction

    A. Sub-Category 1

       1. Story 1

    B. Sub-Category 2

       1. Story 1

II. Main Category 1

    A. Sub-Category 1

    B. Sub-Category 2

       1. Supporting Topic 1

          a. Example 1

          b. Example 2

       2. Supporting Topic 2

          a. Example 1

          b. Example 2

    C. Sub-Category 3

    D. Sub-Category 4

book, you realize that one chapter isn't going to help you with achieving your book's goal and the information you plan to put in it is better reserved for another kind of book, go ahead and cut it out from your book. Or if you think you need to insert additional chapters to beef up what you already have, by all means go back to the library or the Internet and do some more research. An outline is simply a guide, not the last word. It should lead the way but it shouldn't dictate everything you have to do.

Having Outline Troubles?

Creating an outline sounds easy when we put it like the way we did. Sometimes, it is easy. Other times, it isn't. If you know which questions you should ask to get to the big answer, you will have no trouble coming up with the main categories and sub-categories of your outline.

Unfortunately, some writers already get stuck in this part of the writing phase. It might be because they don't have a clearly defined picture of what they want to write about yet. Or it might be because they haven't done adequate research. If you're stuck because you haven't performed enough research, the only solution is to go back to the Research Phase and dig into your topic a little deeper. If you think you've already done enough research but can't figure out how to arrange the chapters of your book in the most effective way, here are a few techniques you might want to try out.

1.   Ask questions.

One of our biggest takeaways from Ryan Deiss, author of *Kindle Publishing Revolution*, is that each book is an attempt to answer a single very important question. It's a big question. In fact, it's *the* big question. Without it, you wouldn't be writing any book at all. And without the answer provided in that book, it wouldn't be worth your readers' time and money to read it. Asking the right questions can help you shape up your outline when you're having difficulties with it.

Ryan suggests you do this by getting a stack of 12 index cards. In each index card, write down one question that you need to answer before you can answer the big question. Of course, this assumes you already know the big question you're trying to answer. We already talked about that in Chapter 3 on choosing a topic to write about.

Each index card represents one chapter. Each chapter should aim to answer that question written on each card. For instance, let's say you're writing a book on developing unwavering self-confidence. Think about the questions about self-confidence that your readers should ask in order to get all the right answers. Next, take your 12 index cards and write down one question on each index card. A few sample questions could be:

- Why do some people have low self-confidence?

- What does the subconscious mind have to do with self-confidence?

- What factors can lead to greater self-confidence?

- What can a person do to build self-confidence?

Once you have a total of 12 questions, you have 12 potential chapters to work with. If you can come up with more than 12 questions, that's fine. Do not limit your book to 12 chapters if you believe you need to provide more information to write a complete book.

At the same time, not all your questions will be high-quality questions. Go through each index card and see which chapters are essential to your book and which two chapters you can do without. Ten chapters all in all should be a good minimum.

Next, Ryan suggests you take a total of 120 index cards. You will need to assign 12 index cards to each chapter. On each of these 12 index cards, write down a question you need to answer to contribute to the chapter's overall idea. Now, flip over each index card and write the answers to your question on the back of the card. Each answer should not be shorter than three words, but not longer than what the index card can contain. Do the same thing you've done with the 12 index cards for the chapters. Answer each sub-chapter question on the back of each index card. Then take a look at each of the 12 index cards to see which two sub-chapters you can do without and which 10 should be included in each chapter.

Take 12 index cards and write 12 questions you need to answer to arrive at your solution. Now, turn these index cards over and write down the answers. Keep your answers as short as possible. You now have 12 chapters.

At the end of this activity, you should have at least 10 chapters with at least 10 sub-chapters. Whenever you get stuck, go over the mind maps you created during the Research Phase and review the concepts and ideas you picked up.

2.   Use deductive reasoning.

In science, researchers use two ways to arrive at a conclusion: deductive reasoning and inductive reasoning. Deductive reasoning is a top-down approach that works from a broader, more general premise (your main topic) to narrower, more specific points (your main categories and sub-categories). If your main topic (the general premise) is true, then there must be several other things that are also true.

For the sake of this technique, it helps to write down your main topic in sentence form. So instead of saying that you're writing about mindfulness meditation, say this:

"Mindfulness meditation is a powerful way to become a better, happier and healthier person."

This is your main premise. From this premise stems a lot of other arguments that are also true. One thing that might come up is: "If mindfulness meditation is a powerful way to become better, happier and healthier, then it must be good for the body, mind and emotions." If this is true, then you have just come up with one major section of your meditation book, the benefits section, which can be further divided into three more sub-sections: the physical benefits, mental benefits and emotional benefits of meditation.

Another premise that could come up is this: "If mindfulness meditation is a powerful way to become a better, happier and healthier person, then you should start practicing it now." You can develop this into another chapter and focus it on how the reader can start practicing mindfulness meditation right away.

3.   Brainstorm for ideas.

When you're brainstorming, you need to turn off your inner critic to allow your creative juices to flow. Too often, when an idea pops into our heads, we instantly shut it down. We think it is too silly or stupid to even think about. Unfortunately, this automatic turning down of ideas is the fastest way for you to not think of anything good enough. So before you sit down for a brainstorming session, remind yourself that everything that comes to mind should be part of your list.

What do you brainstorm for? This method assumes you already know what the main idea of your book is. The problem is you still don't know what to put in the chapters and sub-chapters. To brainstorm, simply think about your main idea and jot down all other ideas that come to mind. Remember, jot down everything. Do not allow yourself to entertain negative thoughts about your ideas. These will inevitably come up on their own, but never mind them. The goal is to come up with as many ideas as possible. The self-editing comes later.

4.   Conduct 15-minute free-writing sessions.

Free-writing is another technique used by writers to generate ideas. To free-write means to write down whatever comes to mind for a certain period of time without pausing to think if what you're writing makes sense. Set your timer for 15 minutes and just write. Don't be concerned about style and grammar issues because no one else will read what you have written except for you. And don't stop writing until the allotted amount of time is up. When the alarm rings, stop writing. Take a look at what you have written and rummage for valuable ideas you can collect from the rubble.

5.   Use clustering.

Another similar process is clustering. It is actually a lot like mind mapping, except it is done in reverse. Clustering is helpful when you want to come up with ideas for your chapters and establish relationships among these ideas. On the other hand, mind mapping is more for organizing information that you already know.

To start with clustering, begin with a few words or phrases in separate circles. Use arrows, broken lines or whatever visual symbol you prefer to connect, compare or contrast these words and phrases. It doesn't matter how long your words and phrases are or what symbols you use. What is important is you understand what those words, phrases and symbols represent. Don't bother organizing too much, though. The goal is to come up with as many ideas as you can and create relationships among these ideas.

Your Brain's Totally Allergic to Outline Writing… Now What?

Following any old college stylebook isn't hard-core. What is hard-core is when you take things into your own hands and do it your way. The most important thing that needs to get done here is to get the flow and the structure of your book down pat. A lot of writers do well with a written outline, but not all are comfortable with it. Some people prefer more visual and more flexible methods of organizing their research and creating their outlines. If you're not quite happy with standard outline writing, there are a few more ways for you to skin the cat.

1.   Create a mind map of your entire book.

Mind mapping allows you to see a visual representation of your entire book. We discussed mind mapping on the chapter on conducting book research, so we will just give you a brief overview of mind mapping here. Because you are working with a lot more material than can be seen in one chapter, it is better to use large pieces of paper or a poster board and several pens of different colors. If you are using mind-mapping software such as XMind and FreeMind, the size of your mind map doesn't matter.

Start with a circle at the center of your paper. This is where you enter your main topic. From this circle, draw several branches or rays that signify your main categories or chapter titles. If you're using paper, use different colors for each chapter so you can get a quicker idea of which topic belongs to what chapter. Off the main branches, draw a number of little branches that correspond to your sub-categories. The number of little branches depends on how many sub-categories you have.

The mind mapping method is particularly helpful when you need to squeeze in a few more ideas into your chapters by simply creating another branch off the main one when you need to.

2. Use sticky notes to create a flexible outline.

When you use sticky notes instead of a written outline or a mind map, you can easily move around the different chapters and categories until you arrange them the way you want. Each sticky note contains one category. It helps if the sticky notes are color-coded. You can use blue for the main categories, yellow for sub-categories, pink for stories and green for examples. Once you've written down all categories into your sticky notes, you can arrange them into a visual outline on your wall or on a poster board.

If you're not happy with the order of topics or when you would like to add or remove a few things, simply rearrange the sticky notes in the order you wish.

Action Steps: How to Create an Outline for Your Book

1. Before you do your research, you must already have an idea of what you want to put in your outline. Once research has supplied the information gaps, you can then proceed to create a clearer outline. The following are the steps in creating an outline.

a. Be clear about the main topic of your book.

b. Identify the main categories. These will be the main sections of your book.

c. Identify the sub-categories. These will fall under the main sections as the chapters of your book.

d. Identify other supporting ideas. These will be the sub-chapters under each chapter.

e. Identify the examples, anecdotes and personal stories that you will include in the sub-chapters.

2. If you are having difficulties coming up with ideas for your sections, chapters and sub-chapters, try the following:

a. Index card questions – Take 12 index cards and write down the main questions your readers are asking. Write the answers on the back of these index cards. Next, go through each question and see the two questions you can do without. Do the same for the sub-chapters of each chapter. Take 12 index cards and write 12 more questions that you want to answer in each chapter. Write down your answers on the back of each card. Then look through all the sub-chapters to see which ones you can take out.

b. Deductive reasoning – Come up with several specific statements that are applicable if your general statement (your main topic) is also applicable.

c. Brainstorming – Generate as many numbers of ideas for each chapter as possible.

d. Freewriting – Write about whatever comes to mind. Somewhere amidst the mess, there is at least one brilliant idea you can use for your book.

e. Clustering – Group similar ideas together. Seeing how all the concepts and ideas are connected to each other allows you to develop big-picture ideas and see things differently.

3. Not a fan of outlining? There are a couple of ways you can create a plan for the writing process without having to create an outline.

a. Mind Mapping – Begin with the main topic inside a circle at the center. Create branches from the main circle where you can write down words and short phrases that pertain to the supporting topics. You can use different colored pens for each branch and close each branch off from the other branches so that you can get an idea of what goes into each chapter more quickly.

b. Sticky Notes – Write down the main topics, sub-topics, supporting topics and other elements in separate sticky notes. Use one color for each category. For instance, you can use green for main topics, pink for sub-topics, blue for supporting topics and white for other elements. Arrange your sticky notes on a poster board. Feel free to move things around when you need to.

10

Rapid Writing

How to Write a Book in 10 Hours or Less

This is perhaps the moment you have been waiting for. At last, you can get in front of your computer and write. There is not much advice we can give you here except to just write continuously and quickly. Don't mind your grammar or your spelling too much. At this point, the goal is to take everything you have in your head and write it down following the outline you have carefully created.

For our first Writers Rise Podcast interview, we interviewed Pat Flynn, well-known Internet entrepreneur and author of *Let Go: My Unexpected Path from Panic to Purpose to Profits*. Pat says: "I've learned since starting out writing books that I need to separate the creative sort of writing process and the editing and making-it-perfect process."

As a long-time blogger, Pat has become very used to writing 3,000 to 4,000-word blog posts with the mindset of writing and editing it at the same time. When he began writing books, he found it almost impossible not to spend hours upon hours writing and editing a single paragraph. What eventually changed the way he looked at book writing was a book by Anne Lamott.

If you're familiar with *Bird by Bird: Some Instructions on Writing and Life*, you would know what Pat means when he says writing is like throwing up on paper. Basically, you just take whatever is on your mind and put it down on paper without caring about whether or not the words you're putting down sound revolting to your ears. "It energizes the creative mindset," Pat says. "And all these amazing things start to come out and are written down and would have never come out before if you have kept double-checking everything and editing things along the way."

And don't think you have to write the chapters of your book in chronological order. If you think it's easier for you to skip the introductory chapter and head right away to the body of your book, by all means do so. You might find it easier to write the first chapter after the other chapters are completed.

Your Sacred Writing Space

Since we can't tell you much about how to string words and sentences together to create the perfect paragraph (but we can tell you much about making sure everything sounds okay in the next chapter), we're going to share with you a few important things to pay attention to when you actually sit down and write.

First among your concerns is the perfect writing environment. Now, some writers can make magic happen wherever they are. They can go into the zone and remain there even when they are surrounded by screaming babies or hip hop music blaring from their neighbor's stereos. But writing is a reflective activity. Most of us can't do that. We need to find the right environment that will allow the mind to relax and focus. Here are some things to consider.

1. The Place

Somewhere you can concentrate is the best place to write. It could be inside your home office if you have one, a small coffee shop frequented by writers and artists working on their own projects, in the kitchen in the middle of the afternoon or at a public park picnic table. Whatever works for you is whatever allows you to keep your mind on your book.

We have some short but informative videos that can help you find the right place for writing. To access these videos, please join the Writers Rise Facebook group and watch the videos for free.

2.   The Schedule.

Obviously, finding time is one of the major hurdles for a lot of aspiring book authors. Most people just have too many things to think about to focus on their book. Both Pat Flynn and Cathy Presland believe that the solution is to set aside a small block of time, maybe one or two hours each day, where you can forget about everything else and work on your book.

"Some people say, 'I have no time at all.' I say, 'Why don't you get up an hour early in the morning and just let writing be the first thing you do when you get up? Before anybody else in the house is up, just spend an hour a day doing it," says Cathy.

According to Pat, "I would only need an hour or two-hour blocks of time throughout the day or maybe at night when the kids are sleeping."

Let your body clock decide the best time to write. If you feel most creative in the morning, write in the morning because chances are you will be most productive at that time. If you are a night owl and like to burn the midnight oil, then go lock yourself up in your home office and write away. If you like to head down to a local coffee shop or if you like writing at the park, schedule a certain day of the week when you can go to each of these places. What is important is for you to have a fixed schedule and stick to it.

3.   The Rituals.

Writers have their own quirky rituals they need to go through before or during writing. Guzzling several cups of strong black coffee before settling down to write and while writing is one thing that a lot of writers seem to share. We know one writer who cannot write without wearing his favorite pair of socks and another who has to brush her teeth, wash her face and put her hair up in a ponytail before she can think. We all have different requirements when we write, but make sure they don't go as far out as renting a special hotel room just to write, just like Maya Angelou does, or writing in the nude, like Victor Hugo did.

The Hard-Core Way to Get Rid of Writers Block

Writer's block has been around for hundreds of years. Surely, even William Shakespeare himself must have had his days-off too. But it was only in the 1950s when writers found a way to give a name to this dreaded phenomenon. It's when you feel like you're stuck and can't find a way to get yourself unstuck, no matter what you do. You stare at the blank screen or piece of paper in front of you and you admonish yourself for suddenly having nothing to say. Writer's block sure is deadly. It can waste so much of your time and can tear away at your self-esteem.

Don't fret, though. There are proven and effective ways to get rid of writer's block. But you might not like most of them. Remember, when you go hard-core, you have to push harder than the rest. You have to go beyond what you think your mind is limited to do. The following methods are not popular methods, but persevering with any one of them will definitely get you through.

1. Write.

Doesn't it seem counterintuitive to tell someone with writer's block to write? How can you write if you can't? Admit it. You can still write with writer's block. You can still put down words and sentences together. It's just that they don't sound as good as you want them to be. Again, this is the writing stage and the goal is simply to put the words down on paper. This is where you take yourself further than you think you can. Just because your writing sounds awful to your ears is no reason to stop writing.

There is another part that is specifically made for polishing up your draft. That part is called editing and revising. Pat Flynn calls it making it perfect. With the help of an editor who understands your message, you can have your draft all cleaned up and refined for you. You don't have to do all the work. You can certainly edit your own work, but most definitely not during the writing part. This is why writer's block often comes up—because writers take on their editor personas and think they have to tweak and re-tweak every single sentence they put down right away. In fact, this process can occur even as you're formulating the words in your mind! If you're not careful, nothing will make it to paper at all.

So go ahead. Write. It doesn't matter how bad it all sounds to you. Just position your fingers over your keyboard and start keying in. Sooner or later, your brain will gather the momentum and shift into high gear once again. By that time, you can go back to the section you weren't so pleased with and write it all over again if you want. Or even better, you can hand it over to your quality department—your editor.

2. Create a hard-core outline.

Lack of preparation is the single biggest reason why writer's block commonly occurs. Research is a very important part of this process because it fills you up with the knowledge you need to formulate ideas you want to write about. It helps you build connections between these ideas. Having an outline allows you to see the flow of your book. It guides you towards the right direction. We cannot stress this point enough. Without adequate research and an extremely detailed outline, you will most certainly get stuck somewhere. But if you go through the Preparation and Research Phases carefully, there is very little chance for you to stumble upon writer's block. But if you still do, consider the other techniques mentioned below.

When you finally begin to write, just write. Don't mind your inner critic chastising you for grammar, syntax or style issues. Just put down everything that comes to mind and do the editing later.

3. Get some expert help.

Sometimes, no matter how much you prepare during your research, it's possible that you may not have covered all your bases. It can happen that you don't have all the information you need to form a complete understanding of the issue. No matter how hard you try, you're still stuck fast and tight. You can do more research, sure. But there are times when the books and the blogs bring unsatisfying results. Take it one step further from the books and speak with someone who already knows what you are trying to learn. A blogger or an academician—the people who are worth interviewing for your book—are experts. If no one can provide the last piece of the puzzle, at least one of them will be able to point you in the right direction to find the missing piece.

4. Think of it as a day job.

If you're not a full-time professional writer, you might come to see your book writing project as an artistic endeavor more than anything else. Yes, writing is certainly a fine art that needs to be nurtured as you patiently wait for it to grow, but don't think of it as something that comes in its own time. The secret of hard-core writers is simple. They show up and get to work. They don't give in to excuses about inspiration not clocking in that day. And this, dear friends, is why only the hard-core writers get things done.

5. Get up and get going.

Being exposed to the same thing hour after hour, day in and day out can get extremely taxing for your brain, even for the most devoted writers. So give yourself a break often and shut down your computer.

A great way to pique your senses once again is to go out and go to places that inspire your creativity. A visit to the park, a coffee shop frequented by artist types or even the exotic fruit farm several minutes out of town may be all you need to get your creative groove back. Or you can take the bus to the next town and try to get lost in it. According to psychologists, wandering in a new place is a great way to increase your creativity. Did you know Charles Dickens purposefully got himself lost around London to free up his creative juices?

Moreover, writing is an extremely introverted activity. Obviously, individuals on the extroverted side can end up really restless and unable to concentrate when they've had too much to write. But even when you're an introvert, it can still get a little lonely being by yourself most of the time. A shift in the types of activities you do can help free up your brain. Studies show socializing can improve brain function. Try doing something a little more extroverted, such as socializing with friends or going to a party. You can always join your favorite online forums, but we think there is no other way to meet up with people than to meet up with them in person.

Another benefit of getting up and getting going is better oxygenation. Moving around can increase blood flow and drive oxygenated blood to your brain and, with it, some new ideas perhaps. The simple act of getting up from your chair and walking around the room or lifting a set of dumbbells 10 times can change your state of mind and supercharge your mental processes as well.

6.   Get off the Internet.

Could it be that the reason for your writer's block is that you've just spent the last few hours scrolling up and down your Twitter feed? The Internet is undoubtedly the world's biggest distraction for anybody trying to concentrate. We find it much worse than a police siren wailing in front of the house and never going away. Sure, the Internet is definitely one of the best places to do your research, but once you get your outline down pat and you're ready to write, get off the Internet and write in peace.

What Cathy Presland does is she takes her iPad and goes off to a café that intentionally does not offer Wi-Fi for its customers. "I can't get emails. I can't go on Facebook. It's like compulsorily cutting off my communication because social media is so tempting just to check out," she says. By the same token, switch off the TV, hang up the phone, turn off all sorts of alerts (mail alerts, SMS alerts, etc.), and eliminate all other forms of distraction that will take your mind off writing.

7. Rethink your outline.

If there is one part that really bothers you (i.e. what you've written makes no sense whatsoever), maybe it's time to take a look back at your outline to see if it needs a makeover. Remember that an outline is a flexible thing. It's not something you have to stick with forever. If you realize that it's better to move things around, do so. You might be stuck because that particular chapter isn't important at all or because you failed to establish the connection between that chapter and the previous one. Go back to your outline and find out where you've gone wrong.

8. Skip the part.

Okay, so you have gone through your outline and you've checked and double-checked. Nothing seems to be wrong with it. You're just having a massive case of unforgiving writer's block. The good thing about writing non-fiction, though, is that, unlike with fiction, you can jump ahead and write other chapters if you want to. Writer's block is really no excuse since you can easily skip one chapter and go back to it once you think you are ready to give it another try.

9. Write on a piece of paper.

This is for writers who like to work on their computer, which is probably the majority of people reading this book. Writing onscreen gives you the feeling that your first draft is already the final draft. That is a dangerous feeling you have to ward off. That neat and formatted look can fool your brain into thinking you have to write the first draft to perfection. And that means you might not be able to write anything at all. Grab a yellow pad and your favorite pen instead. See if you can come up with anything by going old school. You might feel less anxious when you're writing with a pen and paper because there's no way anything hand-written feels like a final draft.

There are several ways to deal with writer's block. All of those we mentioned above are effective methods for freeing yourself from what writers fear the most. However, writer's block should really be no problem if you intend to hire an editor. And you should. It's a must for every aspiring book author to find a good editor because it's the only way around writer's block. Cathy Presland says, "My recommendation for getting over that perfectionism is working with an editor." If you get really stuck, delegate the task to your editor. Ask her to help you write this section. A good editor will not hesitate to work on improving your manuscript.

Write Like You're On a Writing Marathon

Let's set things straight. Before we start churning out the numbers, we're going to be clear with you that how much you should write each day depends solely on your ability to write quickly and effectively. You can write as much as 5,000 words or as little as 500 words each day. That is all up to you as long as you commit yourself to writing a certain number of words every single day until your daily pieces magically transform themselves into a draft that is ready for editing.

We expect that there will be some limitations to how much time you can spend on writing every day, so we'll be using an example where you write for only one hour each day. That's only one out of 24 hours a day, but you can still easily come up with 1,250 words every day. How did we come up with that number? Here's the math. The average person can type 40 words per minute. Assuming you can type at an average speed, you can type 1,250 words in a little more than half an hour, or 31 minutes and 15 seconds to be exact.

That means you still have approximately another 30 minutes to do everything else, that is, setting up your work space, performing your writing rituals, studying your outline, etc. If you can type faster than 40 words per minute, then you can still reduce your working time.

This all assumes that you're going to write without stopping and without giving in to distractions, prioritizing your cat's needs and succumbing to writer's block. If you're committed to finishing your book and you've done all the necessary preparations to make sure you're all set to write, then aiming for 1,250 words for an hour each day should be a piece of cake.

Of course, this is only a quantitative measure of how productive you can be. Do not let the number of hours dictate how you are supposed to do your work. What is important is not how many hours you work, but that you constantly keep adding to your draft. You can choose to write for half an hour each day to meet the 1,250 mark or you can write four hours if you have time and get more work done.

Remember that the only thing you have to do at this point is to get the words down on paper. You have a lot of time to be critical later. Better yet, you can let your editor do that for you. Following this method, you shouldn't have much difficulty reaching your target word count every day.

Here's an Even Faster Way to Write Your Book

If you think writing 1,250 words in half an hour is impressive, what would you think of writing 3,600 words in that same amount of time? Not even the fastest writers can get that amount of words down on paper in so short a time, but you can do it. We'd like to share a secret with you. You don't have to write your book; you can speak it. It's so simple that few people have actually thought about it. Besides, it's the perfect solution to people who feel like they don't have the talent to write their own book but want to become a published author. You can speak your book, have it transcribed by professional transcription providers and send it to your editor for polishing.

The average person can speak 120 words per minute. That's three times more than the number of words you can write for the same period of time. If you only have half an hour for "writing" time, you can produce 3,600 words each day. If you use this method, you can write more or less a 120-page book in less than 10 days with just half an hour of work done each day or a 250-page book in less than 20 days. Compare that with how long it will take to write the same book by writing 1,250 words every day. You will take exactly 48 days or almost two months to finish your book.

Speaking your book will definitely save you a huge chunk of time and get results in a much shorter span of time. If you're skeptical about this method, that's okay. But we encourage you to give it a try because it's simply the easiest, fastest way to write your first draft. In fact, this was what Al did to write *Cheeseburger Abs*, with a slight bit of modification—nothing you can't do. Take a look at Al's writing process, which he describes in clear detail below.

I want to get as comfortable as possible. Before everything else, I pour myself a cup of coffee or hot chocolate or a glass of merlot depending on my mood that day. Next, I get a comfy chair with some cushions and perhaps a light blanket when it's cold. Now that that's done, I plug my headset into my laptop and open my speech recognition software. I also have a voice recorder that is separate from my laptop. I then take out my very detailed outline, kick back and relax on the chair. With coffee, chocolate or merlot in hand and headset over ears, I'm good to go.

I then imagine a good friend or my target reader sitting in front of me. With speech recognition and my voice recorder running, I discuss my outline from beginning to end. I don't want to miss any important point so I have my outline with me all the time. I speak my message from beginning to end without thinking about editing it. It's so much easier to avoid the perfectionism plague with this method. I used to do this while looking at my computer. It wasn't very productive because I got extremely annoyed when I saw the speech recognition wasn't picking up on exactly what I wanted to say. I would say "pretty it up" and the darn computer types out "pretty eight opt." When I notice things like this, I would go back, highlight the words, speak them over again, insert them into the text and pretty it up. But this took a long time. It was distracting. And my writing was taking much longer than I wanted to.

The solution was easy. I just had to stop looking at the computer screen. Now, I don't care what words come out. It'll be close enough. This is why I got a voice recorder. I can play the recording as I go over the text. When I need to make corrections, I simply pause the recorder, make the changes and continue. Where I need to cite my research, I make voice notes separated from the main text with brackets. This is what I do to end up with a complete, albeit extremely rough, first draft.

From here, you can fire off your rough draft to a competent editor. She can then run through the series of drafts to come up with something beautiful. Of course, you can also edit it yourself. Just remember to put it away for a while then come back with a fresh head. The point is you now have a complete first draft. It will take no time to do this if you have a good outline and do the same as I do.

I wrote this section of the book. The rough draft was around 900 words. It took me around 10 minutes to "write" it. I had another 10 to 15 minutes or so listening to the audio version to make the corrections. That's less than half an hour to write 1,000 words, ready for our editor in a rather quick period of time. This is how I do almost all of my writing now. After reading this, you now can too.

Action Steps: How to Write Your Book Quickly

1. Find your ideal writing space. This could be anywhere, in your home office, at a coffee shop or even on a park bench. It doesn't matter as long as you can sit down quietly and write.

2. Set a certain date and time for you to write. You don't have to write four or more hours a day, especially if you have a handful of other obligations to take care of. Just writing continuously for one or two hours each day can help you complete your book more quickly than you expect.

3. Identify any rituals you might want to engage in before writing. These are unique to each writer and must be followed religiously if you want your mind to be at ease when you begin writing.

4. With a voice recorder and your detailed outline in hand, speak your book. Make sure you have voice recognition software fired up. This takes less than half the time it takes to write a first draft.

5. If you're plagued by writer's block, there are several ways for you to handle the situation.

a. Keep on writing. This is the best and only solution to writer's block.

b. Learn to look at your book writing project as a day job instead of an artistic feat.

c. Close yourself off from all distractions. The Internet, among other things, won't help you get far. Hanging up the phone, turning off the TV and putting your mobile phone in silent mode will also help.

d. If you're really stuck, you might want to check out your outline to see if tweaking it a bit can help you get moving again.

e. Give up on the chapter that's delaying you and skip to the next part.

f. If all else fails, take out your pen and a piece of paper and write the old-fashioned way.

11

How to Open Your Book with a Proverbial Bang

And Close with a Thunderclap

The two most significant parts of a book and of any chapter in that book are the beginning and the ending. The middle chapters, which comprise the body of your book, are also important because they contain your book's meat and bones. However, it is in the first few lines of each book and each chapter where your readers decide whether to go further or to put the book down. Accordingly, it is also in the last line where you create a lasting impression on your readers so they will remember you forever.

The Three Elements of a Hard-Core Introductory Chapter

The ultimate purpose of an introduction is to make a promise. The reader holds on to this promise as he reads your book until the promise is fulfilled. Any writer who doesn't bother with writing a good introduction can't expect his readers to go past the first few sentences without closing the book and putting it down in boredom. In other words, the introduction is your first and only chance to make a positive first impression. Don't pass up this chance because people might never pick up your book again.

A good book introduction goes beyond attracting attention, though. It also gives your readers a good idea of what is going to be covered in your book. By the time your readers finish reading the first chapter, they should be able to identify the main topic of your book, why you want to talk about it and how you will go about discussing the topic in the middle chapters. This is the part where your readers decide whether they should put the book down or continue reading.

For many writers, the introduction is the most difficult part of a book to write. It can be daunting even to think about it when you know you're handling such a delicate thing. Get it wrong once and you may never get a second chance to mend your ways. That is, until you decide to write your book's second edition or your second book. But do you really want your first book to be a flop? Nobody wants to have a failure for a first book. This is why you should pay double attention to what you are writing, especially in the introduction.

The introductory chapter typically has three parts: the background, the problem and the proposed solution. Again, this is simply the typical approach to writing an introduction. If you don't want to be typical, good for you. Go ahead and do what you think is the most effective way to put your message across. But any decent book will always have these three.

The background is where you set the context of the entire book. This is where you create a connection with your readers by painting a picture that both you and your readers can visualize and relate to. A book about natural acne treatments, for example, might start well with your own personal anecdote about how you suffered from acne for years. You have purchased every bottle of cream and serum at the drugstore and went to dermatologist after dermatologist, only to have the acne persist on your face. Unfortunately, even doctors cannot exactly pinpoint the cause of acne, which must be why they can't tell you how to cure yours. Surely, a lot of readers will be able to relate to this story because they share the same experiences.

Once you get your readers nodding, "Hey, that's what I've experienced too," mention the problem you want to address. The problem is that a lot of people still suffer from acne even after consulting with skin care experts because they normally don't address the underlying causes of acne. Presenting a problem is extremely important. Without a problem

> *The first chapter's ultimate purpose is to offer a promise that needs to be fulfilled by the time the reader reaches the conclusion.*

that needs a solution, there is really no reason for you to write a book at all. So think of a problem and present it to your readers in your introductory chapter.

When you've got a problem, don't just stand there and whine with your readers. They are reading your book because they think you know something that will solve their problem once and for all. Here is where you give your readers a short explanation of your solution. In this example, the solution is to use natural and organic substances to treat acne problems. Tell them why you think your solution is going to be effective and give them a brief overview of what you're going to discuss throughout the rest of the book.

Six Ways to Write a Captivating First Paragraph

The first few sentences of your book are particularly crucial. While you can have more leeway in writing the first chapter as a whole, it is of utmost importance that you pour your heart and soul into crafting the first few sentences.

There are a number of techniques for you to come up with similar first lines. These are tried-and-tested introduction-writing techniques. They have been known to work in varying situations and used by different writers. However, what works for one writer and one situation may not work for another, so be very careful about which technique you use for opening your book and each chapter within it.

1. Ask a question.

Questions pique curiosity. They get people thinking. Questions make people want to know more about the answers. Asking the right questions at the beginning of your book will definitely pull your readers in. There are, of course, the wrong kinds of questions. These are the questions people don't even bother thinking about.

Take a look at this question: "Are you worried about global warming?" It isn't much of an introduction because we know that people are generally worried about global warming. There are those who care a lot and there are those who don't give a damn at all. But most of us would be concerned if the northern ice caps melted and drowned us all.

Also, so many authors have written about global warming before that you need to ask more than a boring question to stand out from the crowd. "What if, by the year 2020, Florida would no longer be there?" Now, that is one question people probably have not thought of before.

2. Tell a story.

People love stories. We love telling them and we love listening to them. Storytelling has its roots as far back as ancient history, when our ancestors sat around fires and shared stories about their adventures with saber-tooth tigers and other wild animals. It quickly developed into written form but people love reading stories all the same. Take advantage of that. Just because you're writing a non-fiction book doesn't mean you can't be creative about how you begin your first chapter. And it also helps if you pepper the middle chapters with little stories here and there to keep your book from falling into a monotonous drone.

You can tell a story about anything. That is, anything you can always relate back to your topic. You can begin with your own story. Tell your readers about how you began, the challenges that got in your way and how you finally succeeded. Or you can tell short fables that lead to the main lesson you want to portray, anecdotes you've read in the news or you can even make up your own. Stories are powerful because stories add a human element. Don't be afraid to tell them. Remember, facts tell, stories sell.

3.   Employ the shock factor.

The first sentence is normally the only part of your book where it's perfectly acceptable to shock your readers into wanting to read more. However, be careful about overdoing it. There are some writers who can get away with shocking the senses out of their readers chapter after chapter. But you can't simply spring surprise after surprise on your readers, or else they get tired of your shock tactics and move on to the next comfortable read.

One good way to do this at the beginning of your book is to state a surprising fact. "Yes, you can tickle yourself. The only place you can tickle yourself is at the top of your mouth. Try it." Without a doubt, you will have hordes of readers trying to tickle the top of their mouths with their tongues. Congratulations! You have them hooked. Just make sure you can transition smoothly from your surprising introduction into more level-headed sub-chapters where you talk about the background of your book, the problem you want to solve and the solution you offer.

4.   Use original metaphors.

When you put together two things that normally don't belong together, you have to establish a unique connection between them. When you do that, you succeed in making an impression in your readers' minds because you show them that your book is going to be different.

Here are a few examples to get you thinking:

• Going on the Internet is landing on the moon.

• Friendship is a bowl of chicken soup.

• The past is the future.

• Computers are the black holes of our universe.

• We are gold fish swimming in a silver bowl.

The challenge of using metaphors like these is for you to be able to explain what it means in the following paragraphs and relate the metaphor to the main topic.

For instance, you can say that it has always been man's ultimate dream to land on the moon. Being able to step on that orb of white light hanging in the night sky has always signified for us the ability to do everything we always wanted to do. This dream was realized by Neil Armstrong when he made the first human step on the moon. For us ordinary mortals, however, we still have to experience that ultimate freedom and success of landing on the moon. Could it be that the Internet offers us the chance for that ultimate freedom and success? Or something like that. This will get you thinking about how going online is similar to reaching the moon.

Go on and flesh out the metaphor you want to use. Explore how it is going to naturally connect with the topic of your book. Introductions like these are valuable because they incite wonder and make it easier for you to make a lasting impression.

5.   Keep it funny.

When done appropriately, funny first lines and stories can really hook readers in. Most of us have had too much of the stiff, formal tones of language we usually work with when in school or at the office. You will be giving your readers a much needed breath of fresh air when you open your book with a joke. It shows you're not afraid of letting your hair down and you can take things lightly.

A word of warning for the uninitiated, though: Jokes should be treated carefully. Do not, under any circumstance, make a joke at the expense of another gender, another race, people belonging to a certain religion or any other kind of joke that may offend groups of people. Keep it clean and healthy. If you can't, avoid trying to be funny altogether.

6.   Use quotations.

Actress Marlene Dietrich said, "I love quotations because it is a joy to find thoughts one might have beautifully expressed with much authority by someone recognized wiser than oneself." Marlene Dietrich said it all. Sometimes, the things you want to say have already been said, and there is no way for you to say it even better.

The key to choosing the right quotation for your opening is to find one that hasn't been used by everyone else in the past. Most clichés may be true but they are never a good way to start anything. It is best to avoid quotations that people have become too familiar with. How many times have you read the following quotations in amateur essays?

- "Be the change you want to see in the world." – Mahatma Gandhi

- "You only live once." – Mae West

- "You've gotta dance like nobody's watching, love like you'll never get hurt, sing like there's nobody listening and live like it's heaven on Earth." – William W. Purkey

If you want readers to pay attention, you have to come up with more than a hackneyed old saying that has been used so many times it has lost all meaning, however meaningful it used to be.

It's a Wrap! Six Steps to Write that Crucial Concluding Chapter

Despite all we've said about having a phenomenal first chapter, the ending of your book is even more important than its beginning. Have you ever gone to the movies and seen a film that got you yawning at its opening lines but had you at the edge of your seat by the time it ended? How did you find the movie? If you were grossly entertained and clamoring for more when the credits began rolling, chances are you liked the movie a lot, even if the beginning was a little dull.

That is how it is with books as well. If your readers decide to go through a passable excuse for an introduction right to the body and ending of your book, then you will have to get everything right so that the ending will be more than just passable. Every writer wants his book to be remembered, and the best way to do that is to finish strongly so that the words and the emotions that were stirred up by those words remain. Here are a few tips on how you can accomplish that.

1.   Read your first draft.

This is especially useful if it took you quite some time to get to the ending because you need to refresh your memory on what has been already written. As you go through your first draft, take a look at the important turning points and jot them down. These are the points that need to be emphasized in the last chapter because they are what you want your readers to remember after they've closed the book.

2. Go back to the beginning.

Read your introductory chapter again to see how you can connect it to your last chapter and bring your book to full circle. Is there an anecdote that could be useful again in the last chapter? Is it worth reiterating the quotation you mentioned before? More importantly, are there new insights that you can share using the same anecdote or quotation?

3. Present a conclusion.

All the ideas presented in the preceding chapters work together to build up the main point of your book. In the last chapter, you show your readers how these ideas fit together like the pieces of a puzzle so that your conclusion makes sense. This is not the place for you to throw in a surprising statistic or offer another argument to support your point. The shock factor works well usually only in introductions and the arguments should be discussed one by one in the body of your book. The ending is where you tie things up together and close on a strong note.

4. Play up the significance of your book.

If you haven't already done so in the first chapter, the last chapter is where you explain to your readers the importance of the information they have just read. What does it all have to do with your readers' lives? How can they apply their newly-gained knowledge to solve their problems, address their fears and make their lives better? Turning a spotlight on the benefits they can get out of your book in the last chapter reminds them that it was worth buying and reading. This is important if you want your readers to learn from your book and apply the lessons they gained from it.

5.   Push your readers to action.

Whatever it is you want them to do, whether you want your readers to get up from the couch and start moving or visit your website and buy your products, the last chapter is where you want to motivate your readers to do it. This is not the time to play nice and unassertive. Don't say "It would be nice if you…" or "If you have the time…" Tell them in the most straightforward manner what they should do next. People don't like getting ordered around in person, but when you issue a plain-faced, straight-up written command, you hold more power over them than you know.

6.   End when you're supposed to.

Say your last words and stop. Don't say your goodbye more than once because readers will think you're wishy-washy about what you want to say. When you feel like you've written all there is to write, make your full stop and end. And don't be tempted to add a postscript.

Action Steps: How to Write a Strong Introduction

1. Write a first chapter that has these three elements:

   a. A background that explains why you decided to write your book

   b. An introduction to the problem that you are attempting to solve

   c. An introduction to the solution to the problem

3. Experiment with various techniques in writing your introductory paragraph. Choose from any of the following or create your own technique:

   a. Ask a question.

b. Tell a story.

c. Share an interesting fact.

d. Use a metaphor.

e. Tell a joke or a funny anecdote.

f. Use a quotation.

Action Steps: How to Write a Lasting Conclusion

1. When writing your wrapping-up chapter, it helps if you go through your entire first draft again and take a look at what you have written so far. This helps you create a conclusion that nicely covers everything that has been said.

2. Remember what elements you used at the beginning of the chapter and incorporate them into the last chapter so that your book goes full circle.

3. Offer a clear and definitive conclusion.

4. Emphasize how your readers can benefit from your solutions.

5. Create a call to action.

6. End with a definitive goodbye.

12

Embrace Your Inner Critic Now!

It's Time to Edit to Perfection

"It's a fantastic book, with the exception that I had to dodge dangling participles, ran over run-on sentences, battled broken English, and fought with fragmented sentences."

Give yourself another congratulatory pat on the back. Seriously, reach your hand out over your back and pat yourself. You have just successfully gone through one of the most hard-core steps of the writing process. Isn't it surprising to realize that you can quickly and easily create your first draft in very little time? It takes courage to finally get those first few words out, but once you get the words streaming out, you'll realize it's almost impossible to stop.

The next step can either be very easy or very challenging, depending on which path you choose to take. Consider this a major fork in the road. You will have to decide whether to take the right or the left turn. Both paths will inevitably lead to the completion of your book, but as long as you have a couple of dollars to spend, one of them will take you there in considerably less time and with much less stress.

You are down to the editing phase of your book. And while congratulations are in order for having finished your first draft, we're not quite there yet. It is now time to turn your rough manuscript into a masterpiece. Without an exceptional product, you don't have a platform for success. A bad book won't give you the results you want. And as there are millions of books already published, you can't just shoot for just a good book. It has to be awesome. It has to be incredible. It has to be magical!

Most writers say this is the most difficult and painful part of the book writing process because it requires reading your draft over and over again. It's not enough to read it once or twice or even three times. Editing means reading all of it as many times as it takes to make sure everything is exceptional in terms of content and structure, style and language, grammar and spelling. Now, we understand that reading your book over and over again can be like constantly watching reruns of your favorite TV show. When it was airing for the first time, it was insanely fun. But when you've already seen the episode four times in the last week, it starts to feel like a waste of time because it's not so fun anymore. But at the end of the day, it is only the best books that create a buzz and generate income. And the best books aren't created during the drafting process. They are made during editing.

Another reason why most writers who edit their own work find it so difficult is because they identify themselves too much with what they have written. In fact, they find themselves too attached to their first draft that they can no longer determine what sounds good and what doesn't. Some writers may be unable to figure out what is wrong with their own writing because they wrote it. If you are going to edit your own book, you will have to turn your inner critic on and face the music by yourself.

Fortunately, though, you don't have to go through the editing process alone. Other people with a good literary eye will still be able to point out the book's weak points. When we spoke with Cathy Presland, she recommended that the best way to go through editing is to place your work entirely in the hands of someone else, someone with the ability to go through your writing and lay it bare for impartial scrutiny.

"When you have a draft, that is not a perfect draft," she says. "I very strongly recommend that people give their work to an editor because the editor will be able to take a view on whether the book is complete enough and whether there are some sections where you haven't expressed yourself as clearly as you could have. Somebody who could take an objective view of your book and say, 'This section's a little bit rambling.'"

Another reason why most writers who edit their own work find it so difficult is because they identify themselves too much with what they have written. In fact, it is easy to find ourselves too attached to our first draft. We wrote it so we become close to it. In fact, it often happens that we become too close that we lose the ability to objectively determine what sounds good and what doesn't. So if you are going to edit your own book, you will have to turn your inner critic on and face the music by yourself.

If you are writing your very first book, it can be scary to hand over your first draft to a professional editor. What dreadful comments will come back to you? Will she cut off entire chapters and sections? What if your first draft was so terrible that she asks you to rewrite the whole thing altogether? Actually, you've just been watching too much reality TV.

"In my experience, usually, our content is better than we think it is because we know everything that we know. And actually, we forget that most of our readers are beginners or some stage behind us, so they will get more out of our material than we might imagine. Usually the editor will come back and there are lots of great comments about the book and a few tweaks or a few changes that you need to make," says Cathy Presland, who works with several entrepreneurs and helps them write, publish and sell their own books.

So take a deep breath and relax. Working with an editor won't kill you. In fact, it just might be the difference between having a book worth buying and a book rotting on the bookstore's shelves.

A Note for Self-Editors: Get Ready!

For financial reasons, some authors might want to do the editing themselves. After all, if you don't have the budget to pay for professional editing, you have to work with what you have. Still, we do recommend that you show your work to someone who can offer valuable feedback about your writing. You might have a friend or a family member who has experience in writing or editing books. Or you can work on the editing yourself but contact a professional afterwards. This way, your editor won't have to do so much of the work because you've done a lot of it yourself.

If you plan to edit your own book, always remember that the writing phase and the editing phase are two separate entities altogether. The purpose of the writing phase is for you to continuously write until you have written the last word. It's fine if you want to correct typos or run-on sentences, but don't keep deleting and re-writing whole paragraphs while you're still in the writing phase. The editing phase is for you to go back to what you have written and watch out for words, sentences, paragraphs and even entire chapters you would like to change.

Once you've put the last full stop that indicates the end of your first draft, shut down your computer and walk away. Do whatever you need to do to keep your mind away from your first draft. Take a vacation, jump into a new project—whatever makes you feel ready to take on your first draft again. How long this takes depends entirely on you. Most people we know said it took them at least a week, sometimes even a month, to mentally dissociate themselves from their book before they can come back and look at it objectively again. You'll be surprised when you open your book again to feel as though you're looking at it through different eyes. This way, it will be easier for you to notice your errors and admit them rather than try to convince yourself that nothing's wrong with it.

Another way to get yourself detached is to open your manuscript in another format. If you've been working on a computer, it might help if

It is always in your best interest to hand your book over to a professional editor. This gives you time to rest and a second pair of eyes more objective than yours to look over what you have written.

you print out your first draft and read the hard copy first. One technique we like to do is to change the appearance of the text. We find that simply changing the font size, style and color does wonders in tricking your brain into believing that this was not the text you were working on for so long. You don't get so tired easily because your brain thinks it's a different draft you're now trying to edit.

And get whatever gets you going. It could be a cup of coffee, a bowl of nuts or a CD of relaxing music. Editing, at least language and grammar editing, won't require a lot of creative thinking. However, your brain needs to concentrate for you to spot the often-missed portions of the text that need to be corrected. Thus, it is helpful if you do everything to keep your brain focused.

And lastly, if you find yourself stuck, or you're unsure whether a particular sentence sounds good, read it out loud. The ears are sometimes more adept at catching awkward phrases than the eyes. If it doesn't roll off the tongue smoothly, it needs to be changed.

Editing Out Content Gaps and Wobbly Structure

It makes sense to start paying attention first to the big changes you might want to make instead of editing for small changes in grammar or style. You don't want to work on refining your sentences and then realize you have to take out huge chunks of perfect-sounding but utterly useless text. And by the way, yes, you might have to take out entire chapters and sections that you dearly love but cannot find a use for in building a strong conclusion.

That's just how it is when you're writing a book. As Sir Arthur Quiller-Couch aptly said it, learn to "murder your darlings." You can take the easy approach. Get some distance between you and your creation by taking the post-raft break and getting a good professional editor. That way, you won't cry tears of anguish because you didn't have to do all the chapter-murdering yourself.

When you're editing for content, the main question you want to answer is: Have you written about everything your reader needs to learn to understand your topic completely and thoroughly? If not, then what other topics do you need to cover to add to the understanding of your book?

Look for the gaps in knowledge and see what you can do to fill in those gaps. You will need to go over your notes in Evernote or conduct additional research if you want to seal in the empty spaces. Look for instances where the argument cannot hold much water. Can you support your arguments with more examples and real-life stories? If you answered yes, then do all the chapters complement one another? Do they flow smoothly together to build up the conclusion of your book? Are the arguments arranged in a logical sequence, perhaps beginning from simplest to most complex, in chronological order or from the first step to the last step? Does your book have a clear beginning and ending? Does each chapter have its own clear beginning and ending and transition flawlessly into the next chapter?

And just as important, are all the facts and data you presented in your book up-to-date and accurate? Now is the time to double-check your information to make sure everything you offer is true and reliable. If you are not sure about certain pieces of information, verify. And if you have to borrow concepts, ideas or excerpts from other sources, cite them properly.

Editing to Replace Faulty Language Use

Now that you have established the completeness, accuracy and structure of your content, you can look a little closer at each of the paragraphs and sentences and work towards creating clarity in all you have written. In this part of the editing phase, you need to do several things.

1. Cut out the parts that don't add meaning to your book.

    We all like to write more than we're supposed to. There is this idea going around that the longer your sentences are, the better writer you are. That's not necessarily true. In fact, if you can drive home the point in fewer words, the better. Take a look at this sentence: "We're going to talk about several of the benefits of using natural, healthy treatments to get rid of acne." This one has too many words in it. How can you trim it down to make it more concise? You can say, "We're going to discuss the benefits of natural acne treatments."

2.   Replace big words with simple ones.

There's also another idea going around that writing with big words makes you look smarter. On the contrary, it doesn't. It makes you look like you're trying too hard to impress, which is not a good thing. If you want your readers to understand what you're writing about, write as if you're writing for a fifth-grader. People have had too much of high-sounding prose at work or in school. MS Word has a built-in tool that helps you assess the readability of your entire document. There are also several online tools you can use for free to do the same thing. These tools can help you figure out whether your text is simple enough to be understood easily.

3.   Get rid of adverbs.

A few adverbs sprinkled here and there to emphasize a point is fine. Don't just overload your book with them. Adverbs are the most useless part of speech in the English language, with adjectives coming in second. Instead of opting for adverbs, choose words.

"He ate hungrily," doesn't have as much impact as, "He devoured every last bit of food in front of him." Or instead of writing, "She danced gracefully," write, "She twirled around, keeping her toes pointed on the floor."

4.   Use the active voice.

Passive sentences are weak. People who want to dodge responsibilities use passive sentences to make excuses for their behavior. For example, they say, "Mistakes were made," instead of fully admitting they made a mistake. That is a passive sentence made by people who don't want to take the blame. To keep the flow of your book moving, you have to incorporate a lot of action. That means you have to use a lot of action words. The active sentence "I made a mistake" definitely wins you more admirers than a passive "Mistakes were made."

5.   Get rid of dangling modifiers.

A dangling modifier is a phrase that refers to something not clearly stated in the sentence. This sentence has a dangling modifier:

"With love and support from family and friends, depression can be eased."

The phrase "with love and support from family and friends" is a dangling modifier because we don't know what part of the sentence it refers to. It seems to refer to depression, but how can depression receive love and support from family and friends? People, not their conditions, receive love and support.

A lot of people make dangling modifiers because it is not easy to recognize them, especially if you're rushing through the text. Many times, the subconscious mind will fill in the knowledge gap so you can go ahead assuming what the dangling modifier refers to. People may quickly understand the mistake and forgive you, or they may not. It is always better to be on the safe side. After all, it is a book you're writing, not a short Facebook status. You are writing so that people can learn from you. For that to happen, you have to make your book easy to read and the sentences easy to understand. You don't want people to read your sentences twice just so they can understand them.

Proofreading for Picture-Perfect Book Copy

Proofreading is what you have a spellchecker and a grammar-checker for, right? Wrong. Having a spellchecker or a grammar-checker do the job for you isn't always the best option because these applications don't always get it right. Yes, they do have several spelling and grammar rules programmed into them. However, language is dynamic and writing rules change a lot. There are instances when what would normally apply in a similar situation won't work as well for yours, or when breaking the rule works better.

This is why you should still have a human reader check your book for grammar and spelling mistakes. Proofreading involves checking for grammar, spelling, punctuation and basic word usage errors. It helps if you proofread for one kind of error at a time. For example, for the first round of proofreading, look for grammar errors first. Don't bother with any misspellings or usage mistakes because you will work on them later.

This way, you won't lose your focus by watching out for too many things at one time.

Go through the text slowly and thoroughly. Running your eyes through the text causes you to miss errors because you're making unconscious corrections as you fly through the text. Read it out loud if it helps. This allows you to listen specifically for poorly constructed sentences you would normally miss when you're reading with your eyes. And, if you're editing the text yourself, get a copy of William Strunk and E.B. White's classic *Elements of Style* to refresh your memory on style and grammar rules as well as John Grossman's *The Chicago Manual of Style* and the *Associated Press Stylebook and Briefing on Media Law.*

You will have to read your draft not once, not twice and not even three times during proofreading. You might have to read it four times or more to make sure there are no errors of any kind. It sounds tempting to ditch the proofreading stage, but you will thank yourself once your book is out. Readers will pick at your book at all levels. They will notice every single misspelled word and every error you make in using your tenses. And they won't be shy about emailing you about your mistakes or posting scathing reviews of your book on Facebook and book review websites.

Content definitely is more important than grammar, but bad grammar and poor spelling hint at one thing: you're a sloppy writer and readers will look elsewhere for their content fix. Don't skip this part even if you've read your draft a thousand times.

Five Tips for Working with an Editor

If you have decided to hire a professional editor, you find yourself at an advantage. It's a worthy investment for any writer to get his or her work edited by someone who knows what he is doing. Professional editing services aren't free, but you get to focus on getting your expert knowledge down on paper instead of ensuring that your writing is 100% perfect. You don't need to worry about that because an editor will do that for you.

Of course, there might be a bit of bias here since we are selling professional editing services at WritersRise.com. But we know no easier way of writing a book and finishing it than getting the help of an editor. You can ask every succesful author you know and he will tell you: Having an editor to help you shape up and polish your book is priceless.

Once you have decided that professional editing is the way to go, consider the following action steps.

1.   Find an editor.

There are so many ways for you to do this. Of course, you can start at WritersRise.com, but if you don't want to, you can always do a Google search. You can also post an advertisement on Craigslist or any other classified ads website. You might also find freelance editors on Elance or oDesk. We recommend that you find an editor who is college or university-educated. If nobody suits your tastes, ask your friends and colleagues if they know anyone who could help. Personal recommendations are worth their weight in gold.

2.   Ask for samples.

When you finally find an editor you think you would like to work with, don't be shy about asking for samples of their previous work. Or you can send them one page of your manuscript and ask them to give you a sample of how they will edit it. Some editors are willing to do this for a fraction of the fee they would charge if they edited your entire manuscript. If you are satisfied with their sample, they can then move ahead to edit the longer document.

3.   Decide on the kind of editing services you need.

A professional editor can edit your book for problems with content and structure, inadequacies with style and language, or grammar and spelling errors. Or she can edit your book for all of these problems. If you feel that you have your content down pat and the structure flows perfectly, you might want to ask your editor to work on the language and grammar of your book. However, if you think your content comes up short, tell your editor and trust her to find a way to work around these shortcomings.

4. Agree on a schedule.

Once you find an editor you're willing to work with, you need to understand what's already on his plate. If you are working with a freelancer, there might be other books he is already working on. This is where you'll find the advantage in working with a larger company because they are not dependent on one single person's schedule. If you want to get your book edited sooner, a larger company can do that for you. So ask your editor how long he will take to finish your book, considering all the other books he is working on, and see if it fits your publishing timeline. Here's a tip for working with schedules: Set several milestones and deadlines. For instance, if your editor can finish working on one chapter in one day, set daily deadlines and ask him to send you the edited chapter at the end of each day. This way, you know how far your book's progress is coming along all the time.

5. Remember that you get what you pay for.

If you're like most people, you want your manuscript edited quickly and edited well. Editing services are no different from anything else. Quality and price go hand in hand. A few freelancers might charge you an hourly rate but you should decline this. There is no way for you to monitor your editor's productivity if you agree to pay hourly fees. This means he can easily claim he put in more hours than he actually did and make you pay more than what you're supposed to.

We're not saying a lot of people will rip you off. We're saying that without a signed and solid agreement to back you up, you might get yourself in a bad situation. The best way to avoid this is to work with a professional service agency that has professional systems and a fixed-price scheme in place.

Action Steps: How to Edit Your Book to Perfection

1. Hire an editor. This gives you time away from your book to focus on other important things and get the edited manuscript back with professional results. When you hire an editor, be sure that you do the following:

a. Decide upon the editing services you need. You might only need editing for content and structure, or language and style. You might only need proofreading. Or you might need all kinds of services. Communicate with your editor what you need.

b. Search the Internet for a professional editor. You can also ask your colleagues and friends for a referral if they know somebody. And, of course, check out WritersRise.com.

c. Ask for editing samples. Some editors will agree to edit the first page of your manuscript for a small fee. This will give you an idea of the quality of work the editor does.

d. Agree on a deadline. A professional company will turn around a 50,000-word (200 pages) edited manuscript in a week or two.

e. Settle on the payment terms and make sure everything is written down in agreement. Milestone payments are okay, but don't agree to pay everything in advance.

2. If you're editing your own work, take a step back and keep away from your book for as long as you need. This may take a while, typically between a week to a few months, allowing you the time you need to mentally dissociate yourself from your book and be able to look at it with different eyes when you decide to come back to it.

3. Get a copy of William Strunk and E.B. White's *Elements of Style*. This classic style book will be your guide when you realize you've forgotten your elementary grammar rules. You probably also want to check out *The Chicago Manual of Style* by John Grossman and the *Associated Press Stylebook and Briefing on Media Law*.

4. Edit your book for content and structure flaws first. Make sure that all main topics are covered and arranged in the most effective order. Some questions you might want to answer are the following:

a. Will your readers thoroughly and completely understand what you want to say?

b. Are there additional chapters or sub-chapters you need to include? Are there chapters you need to remove?

c. Do you offer enough real-life examples and stories to support your ideas?

d. Are all the facts you present accurate and up-to-date?

5. Edit for errors in language and style. These have to do with word choice, the use of idioms and general sentence structure. Things you have to watch out for when you're editing for language and style are the following:

a. Wordy sentences. If you can say the same thing in fewer words, do so.

b. Big words. People don't like big words. It gives off the impression that you're trying too hard to impress.

c. Adverbs. "Happily," "torturously" and "feebly" don't give readers much of a picture inside their heads. Use action words instead.

d. Passive sentences. They take the action and the excitement away from your work. Turn them around and make them active instead.

e. Dangling modifiers. They're hard to find, but readers studying your every move will always notice them.

6. Proofread for grammar, spelling, and punctuation errors. Go through your book once for each kind of error and read the text slowly to make sure you don't miss anything.

13

Title Writing 101

A Crash Course on
Writing Titles that Hook

"We've reviewed your manuscript. It is well written,
unbiased and quick-witted. Sorry, we can't use it."

You don't have to be a rocket scientist to figure out that the title of your book matters a lot. Although the title is not your only marketing strategy, it is one of the most powerful ways to make a good first impression and keep it. Think of your title as the name of your book. People are not going to refer to it as Mr. So-and-So or Ms. This-and-That's Book. They are going to call your book by its title. In the same way as you probably should not name your daughter Zippity Bop-Bop, you should also put much effort in naming your book more appropriately.

But titles, no matter how short they are, are very complex. They are way shorter than the huge blocks of text in your book, but they take more time and energy than any other section of your book to write. The most challenging thing about book titles is that, as Jay Papasan mentioned when we interviewed him, "Titles are very subjective." You could come up with what you honestly think to be the most brilliant title in history, but still find a lot of other people disagreeing. Or you could use a less-than-inspiring title and still see continuous book sales coming in.

Ideas and Opinions is a pretty lame excuse for a book title, but if you are Albert Einstein, you can probably get away with such an uncreative book title. The title of Stephen King's *On Writing* might sound ambitious. If you didn't know that it was written by one of the best horror and fantasy novelists of all time, you wouldn't think *On Writing* might live up to readers' expectations set by a very demanding title. And have you ever heard about *Book*? *Book* is actually the title for a book co-written by Whoopi Goldberg. It's not doing as well as *Ideas and Opinions* and *On Writing* on the bestsellers' charts, but *Book* is amassing positive reviews from Goldberg's fans.

It's no question that book titles are extremely important, but they don't single-handedly define your success. Some people can write a bad title and still sell their book. Albert Einstein, Stephen King and Whoopi Goldberg all have names that are much, much bigger than their book titles. If you have one of those types of names, congratulations! But if you don't, it is probably best for you to invest a good deal of time and energy creating the best title for your book.

When Is the Best Time to Write a Title?

The truth is there is no prescription for the best time to write a title. It is all about your personal preferences. You may subscribe to the school of thought that the best time to write a title is before you begin writing your book. A title that is there right at the start creates a marker that indicates what should and should not be included in the book's content. If you write your title first and the body of the book afterwards, it will be easier for you to create content that is sharp, crisp and clearly structured.

However, the challenge with this approach is it takes a lot of time to create a title. You could go on and on searching your brain for the best word combinations without so much of a draft for inspiration. And this can take forever, literally. If you focus so much on writing the perfect title without starting with the draft, you might end up with a title and no book at all.

How we went about picking the title of this book is to settle on the first almost-decent title that came to mind. It was not actually anything close to *Hard Core Soft Cover*, but it sounded okay and aligned pretty well with our vision of this book when we first started thinking about it. That way, we didn't have to go around and say things like, "Oh, how's your work on the book about writing a book?" or "I'm working on this book writing book right now. I'll be with you in an hour."

We had a name, albeit a temporary name, to call it by. That made all the difference in making us believe that this is a real, tangible project that will bring us concrete results. By the time the book's content was almost finished, we had to go back to the title to make sure it still represented the message we had given across in our content. It didn't. It badly needed some major adjustments and, after brainstorming, analyzing and testing, we finally ended up with *Hard Core Soft Cover*.

A Hard-Core Book Title Creation System

We hear a lot of advice about writing book titles. But to tell you the truth, advice is cheap, especially advice about something as delicate as book titles. Some people will tell you that there are certain word combinations that follow a specific pattern that were tried-and-tested over the years to work. Other people advocate for eccentric titles, believing that using formulaic titles have you end up sounding just like everybody else, which is exactly what you do not want to happen.

But you know your own book best. You, after all, are the author. You know every single twist and turn in your manuscript. You are aware of where the most crucial points are. It only makes sense that you know best when to use a particular combination of words, whether this shamelessly follows a garden-variety formula or defies every piece of title writing advice on the planet. Any advice we give you on this will be fruitless because we do not know what you are writing about.

However, since we promised to help you deal with the challenges of writing a book, we are not going to abandon you during one of the most difficult stages of the writing process. It took us a while to come up with the title for this book, but what eventually helped us sort through the mess of ideas is this very same title creation method that we are going to share with you. Below is a step-by-step guide to help you come up with a creative and compelling title that will help your book get noticed on the shelves.

Step 1: Go to Amazon.com.

In anything you do in life, you want to model success. So head over to Amazon and go to the category of your book. Take a look at the book titles that are currently selling well and start writing those down.

You can write as many titles as you want, but do not go lower than 20 titles. Just take your time skimming through the list of books and note down every title that worked for you. Now, set aside this list as you begin to work on your own book's title.

Step 2: Create a list of words related to your book.

This is one reason why we put off creating a title to after the content is written. You are better-equipped to brainstorm for different words once you have your manuscript pretty intact. Now, what do you want your readers to think about your book? What major benefits do you offer them? Consider the answers to these questions as you build your word list.

Also, place your words in separate columns. The first column is for nouns, the next is for verbs, the third is for adjectives and so on. Do your best to come up with strong, gripping words. You want words that

Any advice on writing a book title should always be taken with a grain of salt. What worked for others may work for you, or it may not. It all depends on you to set your book apart with a title that's unique and original.

hold great meaning for the readers. These could be words that refer to certain emotions, sensations or burning questions. Or you can depict scenes, locations and actions. However, it is important that you do not censor yourself. If a particular word does not have as great an effect as you would like, write it down still. You want to have at least 100 words on your list. This will help you create as many word combinations as possible to choose from.

Step 3: Browse your list.

See if you can come up with one word that completely represents the message you want to put across. Single-word titles are potentially your most powerful weapon, provided they aptly and fully describe what you want to say. You can create a new word by putting together two or more words and use that as your title. A few bestselling single-word titles are a combination of two or more words. Take a look at some of these *New York Times* No. 1 bestsellers with titles composed of single words their authors completely made up.

- *Ameritopia* by Mark R. Levin
- *Freakonomics* by Stephen J. Dubliner and Steven D. Levitt
- *Megatrends* by John Naisbitt

And here are a few more one-word titles that, despite their brevity, capture the heart and soul of the book they represent.

- *Oprah* by Kitty Kelley
- *Uh-Oh* by Robert Fulghum
- *Outrage* by Vincent Bugliosi

Step 4: Make two-word and three-word combinations.

If you cannot think of a single word that best represents your book, go for the next best thing, which are the two-word and three-word titles. Look for adjective-noun and verb-noun combinations, two of the best ways to create powerful word combinations that can possibly become your titles. Create a list of at least 20 potential titles using all your word combinations. If you have one-word titles, also include them in this list.

Here are a few bestselling books that make use of the adjective-noun combination.

- *American Sniper* by Chris Kyle, Scott McEwen and Jim DeFelice
- *Hard Core Soft Cover* by Nick Brodd and Al Bargen
- *The Social Animal* by David Brooks

And here are three more bestsellers that follow the verb-noun combination.

- *Killing Kennedy* by Bill O'Reilly and Martin Dugard
- *Crossing the Threshold of Hope* by Pope John Paul II
- *Bring On the Empty Horses* by David Niven

Step 5: Create a list of at least 20 potential titles.

Write 20 possible titles. Use all your word combinations. Then set it aside for at least one night. It's best to let your titles sit for a few nights, though, before getting back to them.

Step 6: Go back to your list of titles.

Now that you've spent a few days away from your list, you can have a more objective look at each title. Pick out the top five or seven titles you came up with and compare them with the titles you collected on Amazon. Do these titles match the tone of your book? At the same time, do your titles have a unique element that makes them stand out from the Amazon titles?

Step 7: Test your titles.

If your five to seven titles pass the Amazon test, run them through several of your most trusted family, friends and colleagues to see what they think of each title. Remember, titles are very subjective. What one person thinks is a snappy title might seem a little clumsy for someone else. See if any single title seems to evoke a general positive feeling among everyone.

Step 8: Consult with your editor.

If you are going for traditional publishers, the publishing house's inside editors will most likely have the last say on your book's title since they have a firm grasp on what kinds of titles work and what don't. However, if you're planning to self-publish, then your editor can only give you advice to help you with your final decision.

Eight Semi-Proven Tips to Help You Create Better Book Titles

For all our warnings on cheap advice, we are still going to try and give you some. However, discretion on your part is required here. Some of the advice we give you is going to be useless. Others will hopefully be helpful. The title you create depends largely on your own personal taste. That's something we cannot and will not try to influence. Just remember that advice, whether it is on writing titles or not, only chases after past successes. It does not ensure your own future success. What worked for successful authors ahead of you might also work for you. Or it might not. When you go the way of others who have gone ahead of you, you just might end up where they are right now. Or you might become just another cliché trying to duplicate another person's success. It all depends on how you conquer your own unique obstacles.

1. Write a title that arouses curiosity and a sub-title that explains.

You can easily catch more attention with a short, catchy title. However, with many non-fiction books, readers need to know what the book is all about before they give the book a second look. Consider the following short, catchy titles of some of the latest bestsellers:

- *These Few Precious Days* by Christopher Andersen

- *Proof of Heaven* by Eben Alexander

- *Those Guys Have All the Fun* by James Andrew Miller and Tom Shales

These titles succeed at evoking curiosity in potential readers. Would you turn your head at books with these titles? We would, but we probably wouldn't give them a second thought because we do not know what the books are about. Very often, authors cannot clearly convey the message of their book in one, two or even three, four or five words. That is the purpose of a sub-title. It allows you to condense the benefit of your book into several words you can give a less prominent place on your front cover. Take a look at the above-mentioned bestsellers with their sub-titles.

- *These Few Precious Days: The Final Year of Jack with Jackie* by Christopher Andersen

- *Proof of Heaven: A Neurosurgeon's Journey Into the Afterlife* by Eben Alexander

- *Those Guys Have All the Fun: Inside the World of ESPN* by James Andrew Miller and Tom Shales

2.   Promise a benefit.

Readers want to know what's in it for them, and they want to know right off the bat. It may not be easy to work in your benefit into the main title, considering it is only usually made of five words or less. But there are many successful non-fiction books that offer the benefit right away. If you cannot easily express your book's benefit in a few short and strong words, that is what the sub-title is for. Take a look at these titles that offer the benefit in their main title:

- *Economics In One Lesson* by Henry Hazitt

- *The Millionaire Real Estate Agent* by Gary Keller, Dave Jenks and Jay Papasan

- *Think and Grow Rich* by Napoleon Hill

3.   Use metaphors.

A metaphor is a figure of speech that compares one object to another object that you would not normally compare it to. Metaphors make colorful text that would otherwise be bland and monotonous without them. When you want to create certain images in your readers' minds, you can create your own metaphor. Jack Canfield and Mark Hansen's *Chicken Soup* series uses the metaphor of chicken soup to refer to the healing effect that their inspirational stories, poems and essays have on their readers. The following are some more examples of bestsellers that were named with a metaphor:

- *The Revenge of Gaia* by James Lovelock

- *The Anatomy of Melancholy* by Robert Burton

- *Women Who Run With the Wolves* by Clarissa Pinkola Estes

4.   Play with words.

Puns, alliterations and plays on established titles make you sound smart and playful at the same time. If you're writing a book with a fun, informal tone, a witty title can help you garner fans. Chelsea Handler's *Are You There Vodka? It's Me, Chelsea* is a funny twist to Judy Blume's bestselling novel *Are You There God? It's Me, Margaret*. We found a few more bestselling titles to inspire you.

- *Miracles and Massacres* by Glenn Beck, Kevin Balfe and Hannah Beck

- *Dude, Where's My Country?* by Michael Moore

- *Your Erroneous Zones* by Wayne Dwyer

5.   Short is not always your best friend.

When your book goes on display on Amazon and most other online bookstores, people only get to see a small icon that shows your book cover. A long title can be very hard to read on such a small icon. Also, short titles are much easier to remember than long titles. However, this doesn't mean that long titles never work at all. When done right, long titles can be more powerful than shorter ones.

See what we told you about the cheapness of advice on titles? Contrary advice can work in varying situations. So you might not even want to listen to advice at all and just do your own thing. Here are some long titles that made it to the *New York Times* bestseller list.

- *We Wish to Inform You That Tomorrow We Will Be Killed With Our Families* by Philip Gourevitch

- *All I Really Need to Know I Learned In Kindergarten* by Robert Fulghum

- *If Life Is a Bowl of Cherries, What Am I Doing in the Pits?* by Erma Bombeck

6.   Appeal to the emotions.

When it comes to controversy, authors are divided. One group thinks that any publicity, whether good or bad, is still publicity. You will still get a lot of press however shocked, maligned or disgusted some people are with your book. Ann Coulter, for example, is one bestselling author who built her name on writing books with controversial titles, such as *Godless* and *How to Talk to a Liberal (If You Must)*. Here are a few more bestselling titles that rely on the shock power of controversy to get them noticed.

- *Lies (And the Lying Liars Who Tell Them)* by Al Franken

- *Give War a Chance* by P.J. O'Rourke

- *The Closing of the American Mind* by Allan Bloom

There is this other school of thought, though, that would rather play safe with titles. Ann Coulter, with her established readership, might get away with scandalous titles, but you might not have your own loyal readers yet. Bad news definitely sells, but when you try to awake feelings of anger, shock or any other negative feelings in your readers, you run the risk of having people associate all that negativity with you. The majority of readers prefer pleasant feelings over negative ones. Most of us would rather feel good than otherwise. Take a look at these bestselling books that evoke good feelings in their readers.

- *Happy, Happy, Happy* by Phil Robertson and Mark Schlabach

- *Quiet Strength* by Tony Dungy and Nathan Whitaker

- *You Can Profit from a Monetary Crisis* by Harry Browne

7.   Describe your book as it is.

Telling it as it is and doing away with all the niceties and witty wordplay can sometimes help you create more eye-catching titles. The following authors are not afraid to tell their readers exactly what they think of their books.

- *An Inconvenient Book* by Glenn Beck and Kevin Balfe
- *A Brief History of Time* by Stephen Hawking
- *A Heartbreaking Work of Staggering Genius* by Dave Eggers

8.   Present contradictions.

Two opposing forces placed next to each other can cause quite a commotion. Ayn Rand's *The Virtue of Selfishness* is a prime example of a title that contains such an obvious contradiction. This kind of title boggles the mind. It raises a lot of questions that the reader will want answered. They ask themselves, "How can selfishness become a virtue?" There is no other way for them to answer this question but to buy the book and read it. Take a look at a few more examples.

- *Freedom in Chains* by James Bovard
- *Liberal Fascism* by Jonah Goldberg
- *The Female Eunuch* by Germaine Greer

A Note on Originality

It is common knowledge that authors must strive to keep their titles original. The obvious reason is that you want to make your title stand out from the giant sea of other titles competing for readers' attention. There is another reason, though, and it is less obvious than the need to catch the eye. There are actually loads of books out there that share the same titles, such as *The Double* by Fyodor Dostoyevsky and *The Double* by Jose Saramago, *A Person of Interest* by Susan Choi and *A Person of Interest* by Theresa Schwegel, *History of the Life and Reign of Richard the Third* by James Gairdner and *History of the Life and Reign of Richard the Third* by George Buck and so on.

If you have time to look it up, you will realize that there are a lot of books that share the same title. From the point-of-view of the author as a marketer, this provides one huge glitch in the marketing strategy. How do you expect to carve a unique place for yourself on the bookstore shelves if you share the same name with another book? The key, therefore, is to create a name that you know nobody else will think of.

The Only Three Things that Matter When You Write Lower-Level Titles

Chapter and sub-chapter titles are easier to manage. Book titles may always be a struggle, but it is easy to learn how to write lower-level titles just as we learn to write great books. Very few people were born masters of the not-so-complicated art of writing chapter and sub-chapter titles. This is why you should not be so worried that you cannot yet craft a chapter title that is compelling enough to invite your readers to continue.

There are only three basic things you need to remember when working on your lower-level titles:

1. You are making a promise in your title. Somewhere inside that chapter, you will have to fulfill that promise.

2. Smart writers have a swipe file. A swipe file is mostly a collection of title formulas that have been tested and proven over time to work.

3. Smarter writers do not simply pick a random title from their swipe file. They understand their readers well and know which title works best for a particular chapter or sub-chapter.

So you see, all writing boils down to the same basic premise of knowing and understanding your readers well. If you understand what your readers are looking for and if you can promise in your title that you can give them what they want, you have them hooked. But of course, the burden of fulfilling that promise rests on you. What's an impressive title with no impressive content to follow it?

The Five Rules of Writing Effective Chapter and Sub-Chapter Titles

Formulas for writing effective in-text titles are a well-kept secret many successful non-fiction authors do not want to share with you. They rarely want to create more competition for themselves. Isn't it funny that something as short as one line of a chapter or sub-chapter title can take so much time and effort to write? If anything, this is a sign of how critical your in-text titles actually are. Some of you might ask why we still have to worry so much about writing lower-level titles when the reader is already reading your book. What you probably don't know is that your lower-level headings are actually a subtle way of marketing your book.

Consider this. You might be fortunate enough to catch a potential reader's attention and compel her to pick up your book and consider reading it. The first thing the reader will do is to flip to the Table of Contents to get a better idea of the book's contents. In online bookstores, readers can often get a book preview, which includes a complete view of the Table of Contents. In your potential reader's mind, your boring, ordinary titles speak of your boring, ordinary content. You just lost a potential reader because you did not put much thought into writing your in-text titles.

The good news, though, is you don't need to take so much effort all the time. When you have a swipe file in your writer's toolbox, you can take it out and scan it to see which particular title works for a particular section of your book.

To understand how most chapter and sub-chapter titles work, take a look at the following five principles that are important to creating in-text titles that will market your book for yourself.

1. Offer each chapter's benefit right off the bat.

Provoking interest in your readers has already been done for you in your book title. Now, you want to solidify that interest and turn it into buying action by showing your readers exactly what they can get in every single chapter. You want to make sure that each chapter in your book contains at least one piece of information that your readers should not miss. If your Table of Contents presents a succession of practical and tangible benefit after benefit, there is no way any potential reader will not be tempted to buy your book.

Take a look at the following chapter titles that clearly offer the benefit right away.

- Swimming Your Way to a Healthy Body

- Asian Herbs to Help You Take Charge of Your Fertility

- 20 Things You Should Do Before You Take Out a Student Loan

2. Start with a How To.

We see How To titles everywhere—in books, in articles on the Internet and, lately, in print publications that have caught up with the need to appeal to readers' need for information that improves their lives. However, don't worry about How To titles being old and overused. The good news is not too many writers know how to write this kind of title to their advantage. We often see How To titles that revolve around the process you have to go through to achieve something. Can you see what's wrong with these titles?

- How to Feed of Golden Retrievers

- How to Market Your Business on Facebook

- How to Communicate with Your Partner

What's wrong with these titles is that they rarely reach out to the reader. Remember the very first rule of writing in-text titles: State the benefit right away. The titles above do not talk about the benefit in any way. They merely state the process that readers have to go through to achieve an unspecified benefit. How do we turn these titles around to get the most out of a How To title? Focus on the benefits. The following titles will certainly get more readers:

- How to Feed Happy, Healthy Golden Retrievers

- How to Build and Maintain a Business-Friendly Facebook Page

- How to Understand Your Partner's Love Language

3. Ask a provocative question.

When you ask the right questions, you trigger deep-seated emotions that can push your readers to action. When you raise these issues, the reader assumes that you, as an author who is trying to sell a book related to these issues, very possibly have the answers to these questions. The key to asking questions is, again, connecting them all to the big benefit your readers can get from reading that particular chapter. Here are a few examples of how benefit-laden question titles allow you to invite your readers to read further.

- What Does Your Dog Want to Say to You?

- Are You Actually Who You Think You Are?

- Why Do Women Cry and Men Get a Drink?

4. Give a command.

People do not want to make things harder for themselves. When there is a way to do something in a simpler and easier way, they would jump at the chance to do so. This is why people, although often unconsciously, like to receive commands and follow them right away. Doing so takes time and energy off figuring out what to do next. They don't have to think about the processes or the consequences because, apparently, it has all been laid out for them in each chapter. The only thing left for them to do is to follow. Here are a few outstanding examples of how command titles work.

- Get Up from the Couch and Run, NOW

- Build Author Credibility In An Instant

- Read. Delegate. Forget: How to Deal with an Overwhelming Inbox Like a Pro

5. Offer a system.

Do you want to know a secret? People do NOT want information. They have all the information they need and all the information they don't need at their fingertips. People often find themselves on the verge of a breakdown due to information overload. Have you ever felt strained by the number of books vying for your attention at the bookstore? Or the number of blog posts in your RSS reader? There are just simply too many posts that you realize you no longer have the time or energy to check them all out.

What people are really looking for is a way to make sense of all this information in their hands. They don't want more information. They want a systematic, organized method to make use of this information in their daily lives. Take a look at how these titles give off that impression.

- The Ultimate Note-Taking System for Students

- A Revolutionary System for Stress-Free Vacation Planning

- The New Rules of Posting Personal Facebook Updates

Special Bonus Alert!

To build a swipe file, you must get hold of all the bestselling non-fiction books in your industry and take a look at their in-text titles. Next, you will have to figure out which of these titles worked and which ones didn't and carefully analyze them. Do you honestly have time to do all that just to create your own swipe file? You don't have to because we already did it for you. Go to www. HardcoreSoftcover.com to download your very own swipe file of effective chapter and sub-chapter titles.

Action Steps: How to Write Creative and Communicative Titles for Your Book

1. Go to Amazon and make a list of all the titles that caught your eye in the category where you plan to sell your book. Set this list aside for a while.

2. Take a piece of paper and divide it into four columns. On top of each column, write Nouns, Verbs, Adjectives and Adverbs.

3. Think of powerful words that can go under each of these four categories. Strive to come up with more than 100 words all in all.

4. Look at your list of words to see if you can come up with possible one-word titles for your book.

5. Create different multiple-word combinations. Write at least 20 potential titles, including your single-word titles in this list.

6. Check your 20 potential titles if they can match up to the list of published book titles which you collected from Amazon.

7. Cut down your list to the top five to seven potential titles. Ask trusted relatives, friends, colleagues, your editor and your mentor for their opinion on each title.

8. The following are some tips you can use when creating a book title.

   a. Write a short, curiosity-driven main title and a longer, benefit-laden sub-title.

   b. Always offer your big benefit as soon as you can.

   c. Use colorful metaphors to create images in the reader's mind.

   d. Use puns, alliterations and plays on established titles.

   e. Create long titles if applicable.

   f. Write titles that appeal to readers' emotions.

   g. Describe your book as you see it.

   h. Offer two or more contradictory ideas in one title.

10. The following are the five principles of creating lower-level titles.

   a. Offer the benefit right away.

   b. Start your title with How To and end with a benefit.

   c. Ask a provocative question.

   d. Bark a command.

   e. Offer a system, a method or "the rules" of how to do things.

Tip: Keep a swipe file of chapter and sub-chapter titles. Go to www.HardcoreSoftcover.com and download our collection of in-text titles to help you start building your swipe file.

14

How to Sleep

And Get Your Book Done at the
Same Time

So far, you've done your research, wrote your book and have the masterpiece revised, edited and proofread to perfection. As far as we can tell, it's all systems go for publication. Your manuscript is now good and ready to be transformed into a published book.

The sad truth is, at this stage, some of you might not even have the first draft ready. Let's face it. Some people were born with the ability to weave magic into the written word. Some people simply were not. There is only so much a book about writing a non-fiction book can do for people who have never picked up a pen or typed any words since their last day in school. We're not magicians. We can't make miracles happen overnight. No book ever written, no matter how awesome it is, will singlehandedly get you writing your first masterpiece.

Do not lose hope! We're not saying that only innately talented writers will be able to write and publish a book. Different people have different talents. And what's good about that is we live in a society that thrives on exchanging what we naturally have for things we don't have. Other people will benefit from your ideas. But, first, you have to find someone who will help you get it out and put it down on paper. If you have an amazing idea demanding to get out and get recorded, and you have no idea how to do it, someone out there can do it for you.

The Smartest Thing You Can Do

As you might have already noticed, we live in an extremely fast-paced world. Business people have to constantly keep up with the onslaught of changes that rush to us every single day. If we fail to fall in step with the rest of the world, it could mean lots of precious time and tons of money lost because we can't keep up.

Time, in this society, is such a valuable commodity. Dropping everything else and doing just one single thing can short-change us. Unfortunately, writing and editing a book, including conducting the research for it, will take time, even if you use all our time-saving and rapid-writing tips we gave you in this book.

The smartest thing to do is to drastically reduce the time you need to write your book by having someone else write it for you. How would you like to work on your book in, say, 10 hours or even less? That's a pretty bold claim to make, but it is certainly possible if you find the right person who is willing to work with you. The best writer you can choose is someone who understands what you truly want to say and can translate your raw ideas into an actual book you can see and touch. But why would you want to ask someone to write your book for you? Here are the reasons why.

1.   Get a book written with the help of an expert.

A ghost-writer won't be able to make a living if he produces crappy content. He can deceive a few unknowing clients into a couple of projects, but he won't be able to sustain a steady income stream if he doesn't improve his service. The best ghost-writers have years of experience writing books. They do this for people who would like to get their ideas out there but can't put good sentences together. Their years of experience have honed their writing skills in ways that reading this book over and over again never will.

We want to make it clear. When you choose a reliable writer, you're not dealing with people who are taking a shot in the dark. You're working with people who know exactly what they're doing. Okay, not all people who say they can write for you will be able to give you great content. If you don't do your homework, you'll end up with people who can't write any better than a second-grader. The Internet has made it easy for people to put up a website and advertise their writing services, but it takes more than a website to become a good writer. We'll talk more about this later when we teach you how to find the best person to write your book for you.

2. Increase your productivity.

If one of your goals is to market your business or build a better brand, you're probably going to be busy. We know the feeling. You can get distracted with all the several other things that scream for your attention. You still have to fine-tune your book marketing plan then see it to execution. You also have to find a cover designer and perhaps a graphic artist for your book's illustrations. Then you also have to get the book's interior properly formatted. You must also have somebody design your website and get it running properly. The list goes on.

If you ever wondered how some of the most successful people in the world can get around to writing a book, well, now you know how busy people get books written. They hire a person to write it. And that might exactly be the reason why they can do so much and still publish a book of several thousand words. One big advantage of having another person write the book for you is that you have a huge chunk of the workload taken care of by someone who has the time and ability to do so. This gives you the time and space to focus your efforts on other things that need your attention.

3. Save time and money.

There are no obvious and upfront costs when you write a book by yourself. After all, you're not paying anything to do your research and write, except for the small expenses of registering at a library or driving to an interview location perhaps. However, the real cost comes in when you realize you put in so much time researching, writing and even editing your book. Only the best business people know this. The amount of time spent on a project is proportional to the amount of money you lost on it. Time is money. To some, time is even gold.

When you write a book, especially for the first time, you eat up a massive amount of time. Just imagine what you could have done for your business with that amount of time spent writing. You could have networked with customers and potential partners. You could have created a new marketing strategy. You could even have launched it. Anything you could do to improve your income stream you can do in the time it takes to write a book.

4.   Work with people who understand the business.

Professional writers don't just write when the inspiration strikes. They write because they have to. They don't have lame excuses about a three-day writer's block or their muse having gone on vacation for a week. Professional writers write because they have deadlines to meet. They have a word quota to come up with at the end of the day. They write because this is what puts food on their tables and is what keeps them alive. There will be no excuses because they know the industry they work in. You can expect the book you want in the time frame it was promised to you when you deal with a professional.

The keyword here is "professional writers". You have to understand that a lot of people call themselves writers. We really have no problem with that. When people write for enthusiasm, they do something to uplift themselves. But not all these people understand what it is to write for a living. They are often the very same people who can write great content when they want to and flee when they're not inspired. When you're looking for a writer, make sure he has lots of professional experience to back him up.

5.   Get your book to reach out to people.

The best writers are great at *not* specializing. They are jacks-of-all-trades who can write to any audience you choose. The problem with specializing is it's easy to get caught up in what you are writing that you tend to assume that your readers automatically understand what you are talking about. You think it is easy for other people to understand because it is easy for you to understand. But you have to realize that you have a lot of background knowledge of the topic you're writing about, while it may be the first time your readers encounter it.

Professional writers know it's their job to communicate effectively. They can easily detach themselves from the topic, even while knowing full well what to write. They are aware of the jargon and technical language you might no longer recognize. They know that to establish better relationships, writing in a language that your readers know and understand is crucial. The best writers are also very flexible. They can write in a particular tone for any audience you choose.

Finding The Right Writer

Finding a writer is easy. You can easily go to Google and look for "ghost-writer" or "ghost-writing services" and Google will present you a massive list. It's finding a writer who is right for you that is not so much a walk in the park. You obviously can't merely look through the millions of search results brought to you by Google. And once you get hold of someone you might want to work with, it takes a bit of investigating to make sure they're who they claim to be.

It's like finding someone to date online. You can't simply believe they're good for you because they said so. You have to find proof that they actually are. And it's also more than just finding the perfect writer. You can find many writers who can come up with material that's technically perfectly written, but you can't seem to connect with what they have written. This is essential because, as the author, you're going to put your name on that manuscript. You're going to own that manuscript and people will call that book yours. Your goal, therefore, is to find the right writer you can build a good working relationship with. The writer you hire must be able to understand what you want to say and how you want to say it. He must be able to slip inside your head, under your skin and say your message exactly the way you want it to be said. That definitely entails much more than searching in Google.

So where do you find writers? All the usual venues apply here. You can begin your initial research with Google,, but you have to know how to narrow down your search so you wouldn't have to spend forever looking through millions of search results. Ask your colleagues and friends for referrals. If any of them had a good experience working with a ghost-writer, they will be more than happy to tell you about it.

If you decide to hire a freelancer, you can put up an advertisement in a number of classified ads websites. Or look at websites like Elance or oDesk and have individual writers bid for your book. There usually are some good writers you can hire for a very cheap price on these websites. However, there is not much assurance when it comes to the quality of the individual's work and work processes. This is one huge disadvantage if you decide to work with a freelancer instead of an established agency of book writers and editors.

If you know anybody who is working with freelancers, you have probably heard of the typical woes about writers vanishing into thin air, time frames extending two more months and clients not being given the attention they need because the freelancer is working on several other projects. We're not saying that hiring freelancers is not a good thing. Not every freelancer will bail out on you. And that's a good thing!

However, it is much more likely for you to encounter troubles if you decide to work with freelancers than with an agency. Working with a freelancer is like working with a contractor awarded the project to renovate your house. You are in the hands of that person's schedule. If he gets sick or doesn't show up, your schedule suffers. On top of that, the output is solely a result of the single individual's abilities and attention to quality. But just like it can be cheaper to use a cheap contractor, it can also be cheaper to hire a freelancer than to hire a company.

But when you find a writer via an agency, you will be supported by an entire team of experts. You might be more satisfied with the more professional manner things are dealt with in a company, especially since your manuscript goes through the hands of many instead of just one person. Having your own project manager who is accountable to you also ensures that deadlines and your quality expectations are met. This can be very valuable if you are a new writer or you don't have much time or experience managing a contractor. An agency, after all, is a business that thrives on satisfying its clients.

A freelancer can run and still find other people to complete projects for. But an agency relies on its ability to make every one of its clients happy. What's the difference? An agency has a brand to protect. An agency with one unhappy client isn't a successful agency. When even just one client complains and the agency does nothing about it, it's all downhill from there. That's why the best agencies will do their best to satisfy all their clients. Plus, an agency has the resources to ensure top-quality content. While a freelancer can definitely produce good content, he has to do everything on his own. Any manuscript you get from an agency goes through thorough scrutiny from the writer to the editor to your project manager until it reaches you. This can be very valuable especially if you don't have much experience managing contractors. Agencies also often have access to a larger set of skills that can be useful and save you time in other parts of the publishing process, such as cover design, layout and marketing.

Lastly, agencies never get to work without a contract. Many freelancers, on the other hand, don't seem to be as focused on this aspect. Once the deal is broken, it's hard for you to go after the freelancer because you have no evidence that he agreed to write for you. Another thing to consider is if they do sign an agreement and they bail out on you, you can file a case against them and seek compensation for damages. Unfortunately, most freelancers might not even have enough money to pay you. In that case, a lawsuit will still be fruitless. If you're working with an agency though, both you and the agency representative sign your names to paper. There is a legal imperative for your counterpart to do the best they can not only for moral reasons but also because the contract compels them to do so. This is a good way for you to make sure you get the highest-quality service you can get from the agency.

What to Do When You Meet The One

Just like with online dating, you won't know when a particular writer or editing company you would like to work with is The One. You may instantly feel drawn to her because of some connection you can't explain or you might notice certain details about her that catch your attention immediately.

But you won't know she is right for you unless you give her a try, or at least schedule a "first date" with her to get to know her better. The "first date" could be done in person, during which you might find it easier to establish a connection. Or it can be done through a video call via Skype if you and the writer live in different places. It's not difficult to set up a schedule that works best for both of you. Time zone differences are merely logistical issues. If two people really want to work together, they will find a common time to talk.

By this time, you should already have had a series of emails with the writer. She, on the other hand, should already have an idea of what you want to get written. The "first date" is where you finally get to see if both of you are ready to take this fledgling relationship into the next level. Here is where the details of the project are fleshed out and you find out whether or not this writer can help bring your book idea to fruition.

Just a number of reminders during your first meeting and the subsequent meetings ahead should the "first date" go really well.

1. Know the writer's style.

    Even before you decide to speak with the writer, you should have already seen a number of the writer's samples and know what kinds of topics the writer has written about in the past. A lot of the best writers can be flexible with their style and the topics they write about, but it is still to your advantage to hire one that has experience writing about your topic and in the style you want.

2. Know what you want the writer to do.

    For a ghost-writer to fully understand what you want to say, then you should fully understand what you want her to do. By the time you

You must be able to connect with your ghost-writer. She must be able to understand what you want to say and write in a way that sounds like it's you putting down the words, not her.

meet up with someone, you should already know the specific action you want your readers to take after reading your book. And you should already know what you would like the writer to do to meet that goal. Do you want the writer to research the entire thing for you? Chances are you have already done at least some of your research and have compiled them for the writer to use in writing the first draft. If you haven't, be sure that you tell your writer in no uncertain terms the kind of information that you would like to be included in your book so that she knows where and how to do her research.

3. Settle on the specifics.

There are a lot of things to decide before your writer can get to work. First of all, she has to understand your goals, motives and your readers. She needs to know what kind of relationship you want to establish and the tone and language you will use to do that. It helps if you show your writer a piece of writing with a tone you would also like to use for your book, especially if you're not very good at describing tone. Other things to settle on are the length of the book, the length of each chapter and the formatting style you want to use. This is also the time to decide upon logistic concerns, such as chapter deadlines, time frames and the payment method. All of these should be specified in the contract.

4. Work with the writer.

It's not enough that you hire a writer to write your book. You have to play an active role in the process too. How do you do that without spending so much of your time? The best option is to hire a writing company that will assign you a professional project manager. It will then be your project manager's job to get you from point A to point Z.

On the other hand, if you are working with a freelancer or a smaller company, you need to give accurate and detailed instructions of how you want to get the book done. You also need to have very regular follow-up meetings where you assure that deadlines are being met. The earlier you do this, the less time you will waste. In this case, you must encourage the writer to ask as many questions as possible. And when questions are asked, you must answer them thoroughly. If you want your book done right the first time, then be 100% sure that your writer completely understands how you want it done.

5. Be specific with your feedback.

Most contracts include a certain number of rewrites in the package, which is great because you will probably want a few changes done after the first draft. That's why it's called a first draft. There will probably be a second and a third draft. If you want to change something, tell the writer what it is you specifically want her to change, why you want it changed and what you want the revision to look like. The more specific you are with your feedback, the easier it is for the writer to make the changes you desire and the quicker you will be satisfied.

Action Steps: How to Write Your Book While You Sleep

1. Find a book writer who is willing to write your book and get paid for the rights to publish the book. You can either work with a freelancer or an agency of experienced book writers, like WritersRise.com.

2. Ask for samples from the writer so that you are familiar with her writing style.

3. Communicate with your writer the goals of your book, the specific audience you want to target and the kind of information you want to include in your book. If you have

already done your research, supply all your research material to your writer.

4. Settle on a tone, language and writing style. If you don't know how to describe what you want, give your writer a sample of the kind of writing you would like her to use for your book.

5. Decide on a deadline and your payment terms.

6. Be very specific about your instructions. If your writer has questions, do not hesitate to answer them in the best way you can.

7. Be very specific, too, with feedback. Once you get the first draft, you will most likely want to have a number of changes. Be sure that your writer understands what kinds of changes you want made.

15

Going Hard-Core!

The Single Most Important Thing to Leverage

In over 150 pages of our hard-core writing strategy, one element remains at the top of our list—time. Time is a tricky thing. The first moment you open your eyes after a good night's sleep, you believe you have all the next 24 hours of the day to your advantage. But the minute you lay yourself down to sleep and look back at the things you have done during the day, many of us realize we didn't have so much time to do everything we wanted to do after all.

But time is what levels the playing field for all of us. Each person on this planet is given only 24 hours every day, no more, no less. Whether you are a billionaire or bankrupt, you are given the same amount of time as the man next to you. If you know how to use your time properly, you hold for yourself an advantage that not even the billionaire can buy with money. This is exactly why we chose to teach you how to leverage time during the book writing process. We are not literary geniuses, and so we can't teach you how to create the perfect combination of words and sentences. We are not masters of the publishing industry and we are not promising that you will become the next billionaire bestselling author. But we are experienced authors who know how to use our time wisely so we can write a great book in a short span of time.

We know how it feels to be in your shoes right now. We have been there and we've experienced everything you are going through. We have gone through everything you will be going through as you journey towards the completion of your very first non-fiction book. We know when the going gets tough and where the most common pitfalls appear. We know that the only way to go at this is to go hard-core. And we also know that reading a book about writing a book is simply the very first small step in deciding to write your book. There is so much more in store for you.

In the book writing journey you plan to take, we hope that this book will be your first resource. Use it to plan your course. Whenever you get stuck, just open the book and thumb your way through any page you like. You will see various references to the methods, techniques and quick tricks we discovered along the way.

And, hey, we've said this before and we'll say it again until you get tired of hearing it. We are not book writing experts of any sort. We are simply two ordinary guys from different parts of North America, one from Kelowna, British Columbia and another from Columbus, Ohio, who took our chances, connected with people who are experts, wrote our first non-fiction books separately, learned a massive lot from the process and are now imparting our lessons to you.

Claim Your Four Hard-Core Guidebooks Here

This is only the beginning of your road to authorship. You're in for so much more, and that is exactly the reason why we cannot easily just close this book without trying to give you even more. We want to share with you four additional guidebooks that will help you during the book writing process. Please visit the following link to get all four guidebooks.

www.HardCoreSoftCover.com

Here is a quick overview of what you are going to get from each of these guidebooks:

1.   Author's Hard-Core Startup Kit

Does it feel overwhelming simply to think about all the little tasks you need to do? We created this checklist for you to help you keep track of which tasks you have completed and which ones still need your attention.

2.   Hard-Core Title Starter File: 29 Formulas for Easy Title Writing

Like the polished leather pair of shoes you wear to a job interview, chapter and sub-chapter titles matter a lot more than you think. You can grab attention with an impressive double-breasted suit, but insisting on wearing flip-flops to the interview may just cost you that job. In the same way, while the title may catch people's attention, you just might let it go when they open to the Table of Contents and see your half-hearted attempts at writing chapter titles.

3.   202 Hard-Core Interview Questions You Can Ask Any Interviewee

The hardest thing about conducting an interview, aside from the part where you have to go out there and actually conduct the interview, is to prepare the questions you are going to ask. Don't worry. We have come up with 202 interview questions that you might possibly want to ask. Obviously, you are not going to ask all 202 questions. Plus, you are going to have to tweak most of these questions to suit your specific needs. However, most of the hard work has been done for you.

4.   How to Avoid Accidental Plagiarism: A Hard-Core Guide to Citing Your Sources and Creating a Bibliography

Plagiarism is the biggest crime any writer can commit. If you are going to borrow from another person's works, then you have to cite your sources properly. There are institutions that have created their own formats on how to cite sources, but these formats have been widely adapted by authors all over. In this guidebook, we are going to run you through with APA, MLA and Chicago, the three most common citation formats used for books.

How We Wrote a Book in Less than 30 Hours, And How You Can Write Yours in 10

This book is all about how you can write top-quality books in less than the 30 hours that took us to write it. But even if you follow the path we laid out for you, there will still be a lot of room for improvement. After all, this is only our second book. Here is how we did it.

Nick kicked off this project by writing a very extensive outline. It took him 10 straight hours to sit in front of his computer and crank out everything we knew about writing a book. If we could change something about this process, there would have been two. First, if Nick had spread out the work over a couple of days, he probably would have been more effective. Very few people are very productive when they have to work 10 straight hours. Also, Nick writes around 40 words per minute. If he used Al's method instead and "spoke" his outline and had it transcribed, he could have easily finished the same amount of work six to seven hours faster.

The second improvement is that Nick could have planned better. His assistant was on vacation when he started writing the outline. But we were both so eager to get started that Nick did the research and scheduled interviews with experts himself. If he had been a bit more patient, he could have had his assistant do these tasks for him and he could have saved himself two hours.

Here is where Al takes over. Al was the project manager for this book. He is also the operations manager at WritersRise.com and heads a large portion of our projects. If you choose to work with an editing company, the hours spent by your project manager would actually be zero hours for you. Under Al's supervision, this book was whipped into shape and polished to a shine.

After that, Nick read the latest copy and gave out specific, last-minute instructions for final editing. It took him around 10 hours to do this, but the truth is Nick isn't the fastest reader. In fact, he's a pretty slow reader and a perfectionist too. This means that it is unlikely that you'll use up 10 hours to do this last the way Nick did. Looking at it this way, it is not impossible that you can get what Nick had done in just 10 hours.

We hope this journey has been helpful to you. We hope, too, that you can now set out to write your first book with the highest level of commitment, determination and persistence. But most of all, we hope that you take action now. Because the simple, unavoidable truth is that long-term success is no accident. It is all about getting the most important things done right here, right now.

At this point, you are geared with practical and time-saving writing strategies that work. All you need to do from this point onwards is to set aside enough time to practice. Whether you can find time to write during the day or you need to get up early in the morning or work late into the night, the opportunity is already in your hands. Use it. It's like what Jim Rohn once said: "Your life doesn't get better by chance. It gets better by change." If you really want to write a book, if you have something awesome to tell the world, you will find time to do it. Don't wait for the opportunity. It's already here. Don't wait for you to have time. Make time for it.

As you practice what you have learned, you will become better at what you do. You will see better and faster results, which will enable you to cash in on your efforts and create a better life for yourself and your family. You are the kind of person who is willing to learn what it takes to get you to the next level. You spending all this time reading this book is proof of that.

We hope to get the chance to get to know you better some day. There are a lot of people who talk but only a few who do. Your dedication is rare and you deserve all the success and happiness you will reap from it. We hope you have enjoyed our book. Someday, we wish to meet you, whether online via WritersRise.com, Facebook, Twitter or, even better, in person.

Until we meet again.

About the Authors

Nick and Al have vastly different backgrounds, skill sets and experiences. Nick grew up in a family of entrepreneurs and went on to start a few large businesses that have generated a couple of hundred million dollars in revenue. Al, on the other hand, started on the factory floor before establishing his own martial arts school and becoming an online fat loss trainer. Nick is a personal productivity champion while Al has received an award for his fitness book, *Cheeseburger Abs*.

Their passion for writing brought them together to provide an editing service for non-fiction authors, which quickly blossomed into an all-out search for the easiest, quickest way to write a book. Information on Nick and Al's research is published on www.WritersRise.com. You can also listen in on their conversations with best-selling authors and publishing industry experts on The Writers Rise Podcast.

www.ingramcontent.com/pod-product-compliance
Lightning Source LLC
Chambersburg PA
CBHW060557200326
41521CB00007B/597